EAT YOUR AGE

OFFICIAL RECIPE BOOK

150 DELICIOUS, AFFORDABLE, SIMPLE RECIPES
FOR EVERY DECADE OF LIFE

#1 NY TIMES BESTSELLING AUTHOR

IAN K. SMITH, M.D.

ALSO BY IAN K. SMITH, M.D.

<u>NONFICTION</u>

Met Flex Diet

Plant Power

Burn Melt Shred

Fast Burn

Mind Over Weight

Clean & Lean

The Clean 20

Blast the Sugar Out!

The SHRED Power Cleanse

The SHRED Diet Cookbook

SUPER SHRED

SHRED

The Truth About men

Eat

Happy

The 4 Day Diet

Extreme Fat Smash Diet

The Fat Smash Diet

The Take-Control Diet

Dr. Ian Smith's Guide to Medical Websites

FICTION

Eagle Rock

The Overnights

Wolf Point

The Unspoken

The Ancient Nine

The Blackbird Papers

To my Grandfather, the wisest man I've ever met, who taught me as a little boy, "What you can't get in the wash, you can get it in the rinse." This book is a testament to your sagacious teachings.

EAT YOUR AGE

OFFICIAL RECIPE BOOK

150 DELICIOUS, AFFORDABLE, SIMPLE RECIPES
FOR EVERY DECADE OF LIFE

#1 NY TIMES BESTSELLING AUTHOR

IAN K. SMITH, M.D.

BOWLAND HILL
BOOKS

This book contains recipes to be used as a supplement to the EAT YOUR AGE program. This is not a diet, rather a companion to the eating program. If you know or suspect you have a health problem, it is recommended that you seek your physician's advice before embarking on any medical program or treatment. All efforts have been made to ensure the accuracy of the information contained in this book as of the date of publication. This publisher and the author disclaim liability for any medical outcomes that may occur as a result of applying the methods suggested in this book.

First published in the United States by Bowland Hill Books

www.DoctorIanSmith.com

Instagram: @doctoriansmith

Facebook: https://www.facebook.com/Dr.IanKSmith

Twitter: @DrIanSmith

TikTok: @theofficialdrian

YouTube: @GetFitWithDrIan

ISBN: 979-8-218-54345-7

FIRST EDITION: 2024

10|9|8|7|6|5|4|3|2|1

This is not a diet book or meal plan. This is a recipe book. A big, fun recipe book full of powerful ingredients that you can consume during any decade of your life. Simple, tasty, convenient, and affordable, these recipes put life in the meaning of EAT WELL and have FUN while doing it.

This book is the recipe companion to the big, main book EAT YOUR AGE. That is the book that has it ALL. You will find in that book: a 30-day customized meal plan for your specific decade of life, a list and explanation of the top 10 nutrients for your decade of life, the best exercises for your decade, a specific but flexible exercise plan, the 7 physical fitness tests you should try, the most important medical tests for your decade, and much more. Use this book with EAT YOUR AGE to maximize the benefits.

The recipes in this companion book are specially designed to follow the nutrition plan laid out in the main book, EAT YOUR AGE. You can enjoy these recipes anytime you want. Immerse yourself in the diversity and flavor profiles of these recipes. Feel free to have some fun and improvise a little. Cooking is about the journey of discovery--new foods, new ingredients, and new combinations of the two.

When you get the main EAT YOUR AGE book and combine it with the recipes in this companion book, you will be equipped with all you need,

to maximize and live your best life and find the happiness you deserve and seek.

Cook well, eat well, my friends!

CONTENTS

BREAKFAST RECIPES

Amaranth Porridge with Pears and Almonds

Avocado and Sardine Toast

Berry and Spinach Smoothie with Hemp Protein

Breakfast Burrito with Black Beans and Avocado

Buckwheat Pancakes with Blueberries

Chia Seed Pudding with Almonds and Berries

Chia Smoothie Bowl with Mango and Hemp Seeds

Cottage Cheese and Berry Parfait

Egg Muffins with Spinach and Smoked Salmon

Greek Yogurt with Walnuts and Kiwi

Oatmeal with Almond Butter and Banana

Overnight Oats with Chia and Pomegranate Seeds

Peanut Butter and Apple Slices

Pumpkin Seed and Cranberry Muesli

Quinoa Breakfast Bowl with Blueberries and Almonds

Quinoa Porridge with Almonds and Orange Zest

Smoked Salmon and Avocado Toast

Smoothie with Kale, Flaxseed, and Chia

Spinach and Feta Omelet

Tofu Scramble with Bell Peppers

Amaranth Porridge with Pears and Almonds

Servings: 2

½ cup cooked amaranth

1 cup almond milk (fortified)

½ pear, diced

1 tbsp chopped almonds

Cook the Amaranth: If not already cooked, combine 1/2 cup raw amaranth with 1 1/2 cups water and simmer for 20-25 minutes.

Warm the Porridge: In a pot, combine the cooked amaranth with almond milk and heat over medium heat.

Add the Pears: Stir in the diced pear and cook for an additional 5 minutes.

Top with Almonds: Sprinkle the chopped almonds over the porridge.

Serve Warm: Enjoy the porridge immediately.

Nutritional Information per serving: *Calories: 230; Protein: 6g; Fiber: 5g; Calcium: 180mg; Magnesium: 80mg; Vit B6: 0.1mg; Vit B9: 20mcg; Vit B12: 0.4mcg; Vit C: 4mg; Vit D: 100 IU; Omega-3: 1.3g*

Avocado and Sardine Toast

Servings: 1

1 slice whole-grain bread

¼ avocado, mashed

¼ cup canned sardines in olive oil

1 tsp lemon juice

Use a toaster or oven to lightly toast the whole-grain bread until crisp and golden brown.

Mash the avocado in a small bowl with a fork. Add the lemon juice, and a pinch of salt (if desired) to enhance the flavor.

Spread the mashed avocado evenly over the toast.

Drain the sardines and place them on top of the avocado spread.

Enjoy the toast while it's warm.

Nutritional Information per serving: *Calories: 320; Protein: 14g; Fiber: 5g; Calcium: 300mg; Magnesium: 50mg; Vit B6: 0.2mg; Vit B9: 45mcg; Vit B12: 8.2mcg; Vit C: 8mg; Vit D: 180 IU; Omega-3: 1.9g*

Berry and Spinach Smoothie with Hemp Protein

Servings: 1

½ cup mixed berries

½ cup spinach

1 scoop hemp protein powder

1 cup almond milk (fortified)

Blend all ingredients until smooth.

Prepare the Ingredients: Rinse the berries and spinach.

Blend the Smoothie: In a blender, combine the mixed berries, spinach, hemp protein powder, and almond milk. Blend until smooth.

Serve Immediately: Pour into a glass and enjoy.

Nutritional Information per serving: *Calories: 200; Protein: 12g; Fiber: 6g; Calcium: 300mg; Magnesium: 90mg; Vit B6: 0.2mg; Vit B9: 80mcg; Vit B12: 0.7mcg; Vit C: 28mg; Vit D: 100 IU; Omega-3: 1g*

Breakfast Burrito with Black Beans and Avocado

Servings: 2

½ cup black beans, drained

¼ avocado, sliced

¼ cup shredded cheese (fortified)

2 whole-grain tortillas

1 tbsp salsa

Heat the tortillas on a skillet for 1-2 minutes on each side or wrap them in a damp paper towel and microwave for 20 seconds.

Mash the avocado and drain the black beans.

On each tortilla, spread half the black beans, mashed avocado, shredded cheese, and salsa.

Fold in the sides of the tortilla and roll to form a burrito.

Serve Warm: Enjoy immediately.

Nutritional Information per serving: Calories: 350; Protein: 13g; Fiber: 8g; Calcium: 200mg; Magnesium: 70mg; Vit B6: 0.4mg; Vit B9: 70mcg; Vit B12: 1.1mcg; Vit C: 10mg; Vit D: 100 IU; Omega-3: 0.4g

Buckwheat Pancakes with Blueberries

Servings: 2

½ cup buckwheat flour

½ cup almond milk (fortified)

1 egg

¼ cup blueberries

1 tbsp ground flaxseed

In a bowl, combine the buckwheat flour, almond milk, egg, and ground flaxseed. Whisk until smooth. If the batter is too thick, add a little more almond milk.

Preheat a non-stick skillet or griddle over medium heat.

Lightly grease the skillet with a bit of oil. Pour about 1/4 cup of batter onto the skillet for each pancake. Add a few blueberries on top of each pancake while it cooks. Cook for 2-3 minutes on each side, until bubbles form and the edges are set.

Stack the pancakes and top with any remaining blueberries. Optionally, add a drizzle of honey or maple syrup.

Nutritional Information per serving: *Calories: 250; Protein: 9g; Fiber: 5g; Calcium: 150mg; Magnesium: 90mg; Vit B6: 0.2mg; Vit B9: 40mcg; Vit B12: 0.4mcg; Vit C: 6mg; Vit D: 100 IU; Omega-3: 1.3g*

Chia Seed Pudding with Almonds and Berries

Servings: 2

¼ cup chia seeds

1 cup almond milk (fortified with calcium and Vit D)

1 tbsp honey

¼ cup mixed berries (strawberries, blueberries, raspberries)

1 tbsp sliced almonds

1 tbsp ground flaxseed

1 tbsp shredded coconut

In a medium-sized bowl or jar, add the chia seeds and almond milk. If using vanilla extract and a sweetener, add those too. Stir well to ensure the chia seeds are evenly distributed in the liquid.

Let the mixture sit for 5-10 minutes, then stir again to prevent clumping.

Cover the bowl or jar and place it in the refrigerator for at least 4 hours or overnight until it thickens to a pudding-like consistency.

Wash and slice the berries as needed. Toast the sliced almonds in a dry skillet over medium heat for 2-3 minutes.

Once the pudding is set, stir it well. If it's too thick, add a little more almond milk. Divide into two servings and top with berries, almonds, flaxseed, and shredded coconut.

Enjoy chilled or at room temperature.

Nutritional Information per serving: *Calories: 270;*
Protein: 8g; Fiber: 10g; Calcium: 300mg; Magnesium:
110mg; Vit B6: 0.2mg; Vit B9: 50mcg; Vit B12: 0.6mcg;
Vit C: 10mg; Vit D: 100 IU; Omega-3: 2.5g

Chia Smoothie Bowl with Mango and Hemp Seeds

Servings: 1

¼ cup chia seeds

1 cup coconut milk (fortified)

¼ cup mango chunks

1 tbsp hemp seeds

1 tbsp pumpkin seeds

In a small bowl, combine the chia seeds and coconut milk. Stir well and let them soak in the fridge for at least 4 hours or overnight.

Dice the mango into small chunks.

Spoon the soaked chia pudding into a bowl. Top with mango chunks, hemp seeds, and pumpkin seeds.

Enjoy the smoothie bowl chilled.

Nutritional Information per serving: *Calories: 330; Protein: 9g; Fiber: 10g; Calcium: 250mg; Magnesium: 140mg; Vit B6: 0.2mg; Vit B9: 45mcg; Vit B12: 0.3mcg; Vit C: 30mg; Vit D: 100 IU; Omega-3: 2.4g*

Cottage Cheese and Berry Parfait

Servings: 1

½ cup low-fat cottage cheese

¼ cup mixed berries (blueberries, raspberries, blackberries)

1 tbsp chopped walnuts

1 tbsp ground flaxseed

1 tsp honey

Rinse the mixed berries thoroughly and chop them if they are larger. Chop the walnuts into smaller pieces if not already chopped.

In a small glass or bowl, add half of the cottage cheese at the bottom. Then, add half of the mixed berries on top of the cottage cheese.

Sprinkle half of the walnuts and half of the ground flaxseed over the berries. Drizzle half of the honey.

Add the remaining cottage cheese, then the rest of the berries, walnuts, and flaxseed. Finish with a final drizzle of honey.

Enjoy the parfait as is or chill for a few minutes before serving for a cooler option.

Nutritional Information per serving: Calories: 240; Protein: 16g; Fiber: 5g; Calcium: 150mg; Magnesium: 60mg; Vit B6: 0.1mg; Vit B9: 30mcg; Vit B12: 0.7mcg; Vit C: 12mg; Vit D: 0 IU; Omega-3: 1.4g

Egg Muffins with Spinach and Smoked Salmon

Servings: 4 (Makes 8 muffins)

6 eggs

½ cup spinach, chopped

2 oz smoked salmon, chopped

¼ cup feta cheese, crumbled

¼ cup milk (fortified)

Set the oven to 375°F (190°C).

Chop the spinach and smoked salmon into small pieces.

In a mixing bowl, whisk the eggs together with the milk until well combined. Stir in the spinach, smoked salmon, and crumbled feta cheese.

Grease a muffin tin with a little oil or use muffin liners. Pour the egg mixture evenly into 8 muffin cups.

Place the muffin tin in the preheated oven and bake for 20 minutes, or until the egg muffins are set in the center and lightly golden on top.

Let the muffins cool for a few minutes before serving.

Nutritional Information per serving: Calories: 220; Protein: 16g; Fiber: 1g; Calcium: 150mg; Magnesium: 30mg; Vit B6: 0.4mg; Vit B9: 50mcg; Vit B12: 2.4mcg; Vit C: 3mg; Vit D: 180 IU; Omega-3: 0.6g

Greek Yogurt with Walnuts and Kiwi

Servings: 1

1 cup Greek yogurt (plain, low-fat)

1 kiwi, peeled and sliced

1 tbsp chopped walnuts

1 tsp chia seeds

1 tbsp pumpkin seeds

Peel the kiwi using a knife or vegetable peeler, then slice it into thin rounds or half-moon shapes, depending on your preference.

In a serving bowl, add the Greek yogurt, spreading it evenly across the bottom.

Place the sliced kiwi on top of the yogurt, arranging it in a circular pattern or scattered for even distribution.

Add the chopped walnuts over the kiwi and yogurt.

Sprinkle the chia seeds and pumpkin seeds evenly on top.

Enjoy immediately as a nutritious breakfast or snack or stir the toppings into the yogurt for a more integrated texture.

Nutritional Information per serving: *Calories: 310; Protein: 17g; Fiber: 6g; Calcium: 200mg; Magnesium: 90mg; Vit B6: 0.1mg; Vit B9: 40mcg; Vit B12: 0.8mcg; Vit C: 60mg; Vit D: 0 IU; Omega-3: 0.7g*

Oatmeal with Almond Butter and Banana

Servings: 1

½ cup rolled oats

1 cup almond milk (fortified with calcium and Vit D)

1 tbsp almond butter

½ banana, sliced

1 tbsp ground flaxseed or chia seeds

In a small saucepan, bring the water or almond milk to a boil. Stir in the rolled oats and reduce the heat to medium. Cook for 5-7 minutes, stirring occasionally, until the oats are soft and have absorbed most of the liquid.

Stir the almond butter into the cooked oats until well combined.

Slice the banana and set it aside.

Pour the oatmeal into a bowl, top with the banana slices, and sprinkle with flaxseeds or chia seeds.

Enjoy the oatmeal hot as a nutritious start to your day.

Nutritional Information per serving: Calories: 350; Protein: 10g; Fiber: 8g; Calcium: 350mg; Magnesium: 130mg; Vit B6: 0.3mg; Vit B9: 55mcg; Vit B12: 0.6mcg; Vit C: 10mg; Vit D: 100 IU; Omega-3: 2g

Overnight Oats with Chia and Pomegranate Seeds

Servings: 2

½ cup rolled oats

1 cup almond milk (fortified)

1 tbsp chia seeds

¼ cup pomegranate seeds

Mix Ingredients: In a jar or container, combine the rolled oats, almond milk, and chia seeds. Stir well to ensure the chia seeds are evenly distributed.

Refrigerate Overnight: Cover the container and refrigerate for at least 8 hours or overnight.

Add Toppings: In the morning, stir the mixture, then add the pomegranate seeds on top.

Serve Chilled: Enjoy as a quick and nutritious breakfast.

Nutrition Information per serving: *Calories: 210; Protein: 6g; Fiber: 7g; Calcium: 180mg; Magnesium: 60mg; Vit B6: 0.1mg; Vit B9: 20mcg; Vit B12: 0.5mcg; Vit C: 12mg; Vit D: 100 IU; Omega-3: 1.8g*

Peanut Butter and Apple Slices

Servings: 1

1 apple, sliced

2 tbsp peanut butter

1 tbsp ground flaxseed

1 tsp chia seeds

Wash the apple thoroughly and slice it into thin wedges, discarding the core.

Using a knife, spread about ½ teaspoon of peanut butter on each apple slice.

Sprinkle the ground flaxseed and chia seeds evenly over the peanut butter.

Enjoy the apple slices as a quick snack or breakfast.

Nutritional Information per serving: *Calories: 280; Protein: 8g; Fiber: 7g; Calcium: 70mg; Magnesium: 90mg; Vit B6: 0.3mg; Vit B9: 20mcg; Vit B12: 0mcg; Vit C: 9mg; Vit D: 0 IU; Omega-3: 1.6g*

Pumpkin Seed and Cranberry Muesli

Servings: 2

½ cup rolled oats

¼ cup pumpkin seeds

2 tbsp dried cranberries

1 cup almond milk (fortified)

In a bowl, combine the rolled oats, pumpkin seeds, and dried cranberries.

Pour the almond milk over the mixture and stir well.

Allow the muesli to sit for about 10 minutes to soften.

Enjoy it as a cold, refreshing breakfast.

Nutritional Information per serving: *Calories: 260; Protein: 8g; Fiber: 7g; Calcium: 200mg; Magnesium: 120mg; Vit B6: 0.2mg; Vit B9: 30mcg; Vit B12: 0.6mcg; Vit C: 1mg; Vit D: 100 IU; Omega-3: 1.4g*

Quinoa Breakfast Bowl with Blueberries and Almonds

Servings: 2

½ cup cooked quinoa

1 cup almond milk (fortified)

¼ cup fresh blueberries

1 tbsp almond slices

1 tbsp chia seeds

In a small saucepan, combine the cooked quinoa and almond milk.

Heat the mixture over medium-low heat, stirring occasionally, for about 5-7 minutes or until the quinoa is warmed through and has absorbed some of the almond milk.

While the quinoa is warming, wash the blueberries and set them aside.

If desired, lightly toast the almond slices in a dry skillet over medium heat for 2-3 minutes until they are golden brown, stirring frequently to avoid burning.

Divide the warm quinoa mixture evenly into two bowls.

Top each bowl with an equal amount of fresh blueberries, almond slices, and chia seeds.

Enjoy the quinoa breakfast bowl warm, as a nutritious and filling start to your day.

Nutritional Information per serving: Calories: 240;
Protein: 7g; Fiber: 5g; Calcium: 180mg; Magnesium:
95mg; Vit B6: 0.1mg; Vit B9: 40mcg; Vit B12: 0.5mcg;
Vit C: 6mg; Vit D: 100 IU; Omega-3: 1.2g

Quinoa Porridge with Almonds and Orange Zest

Servings: 2

½ cup cooked quinoa

1 cup almond milk (fortified)

1 tbsp almond butter

1 tsp orange zest

1 tbsp chopped almonds

If not already cooked, rinse the quinoa under cold water and cook according to package instructions. You'll need about 1 cup of cooked quinoa.

In a saucepan, combine the cooked quinoa and almond milk. Heat over medium-low, stirring occasionally.

Stir in the almond butter until well combined.

Serve the porridge in bowls, and sprinkle with orange zest and chopped almonds.

Enjoy it immediately as a hearty breakfast.

Nutritional Information per serving: *Calories: 270; Protein: 7g; Fiber: 6g; Calcium: 220mg; Magnesium: 90mg; Vit B6: 0.2mg; Vit B9: 35mcg; Vit B12: 0.6mcg; Vit C: 9mg; Vit D: 100 IU; Omega-3: 1.2g*

Smoked Salmon and Avocado Toast

Servings: 1

1 slice whole-grain bread

¼ avocado, mashed

2 oz smoked salmon

1 tsp lemon juice

1 tbsp capers

Use a toaster or oven to toast the whole-grain bread until it's golden brown and crispy.

While the bread is toasting, scoop out ¼ of an avocado into a small bowl. Mash it with a fork until smooth. Stir in the lemon juice to add a bit of tang and prevent browning.

Once the toast is ready, spread the mashed avocado evenly over the entire surface of the toast.

Place the smoked salmon slices on top of the avocado spread, arranging them to cover the toast.

Sprinkle the capers over the smoked salmon for added flavor and a salty bite.

Enjoy your smoked salmon and avocado toast while the bread is still warm and crisp.

Nutritional Information per serving: *Calories: 280; Protein: 15g; Fiber: 6g; Calcium: 80mg; Magnesium: 40mg; Vit B6: 0.4mg; Vit B9: 45mcg; Vit B12: 3mcg; Vit C: 8mg; Vit D: 160 IU; Omega-3: 1.8g*

Smoothie with Kale, Flaxseed, and Chia

Servings: 2

1 cup kale, chopped

½ banana

1 tbsp chia seeds

1 tbsp ground flaxseed

1 cup fortified almond milk

Wash and chop the kale into smaller pieces, removing any tough stems.

Peel the banana and break it into smaller chunks for easier blending.

In a blender, add the chopped kale, banana chunks, chia seeds, ground flaxseed, and almond milk.

Blend on high for 1-2 minutes, or until the mixture is smooth and creamy. If the smoothie is too thick, you can add a little more almond milk to reach the desired consistency.

If you prefer a slightly thicker texture, let the smoothie sit for a few minutes to allow the chia seeds to absorb some liquid.

Pour the smoothie into two glasses and enjoy it fresh as a nutrient-rich, fiber-packed breakfast or snack.

Nutritional Information per serving: *Calories: 190; Protein: 4g; Fiber: 7g; Calcium: 300mg; Magnesium: 80mg; Vit B6: 0.2mg; Vit B9: 90mcg; Vit B12: 0.6mcg; Vit C: 25mg; Vit D: 100 IU; Omega-3: 2g*

Spinach and Feta Omelet

Servings: 1

2 eggs

½ cup fresh spinach, chopped

1 tbsp feta cheese, crumbled

1 tbsp milk (fortified with calcium and Vit D)

1 tsp olive oil

Wash and chop the fresh spinach.

Crack the eggs into a bowl, add the milk, and whisk together until well combined.

Heat the olive oil in a non-stick skillet over medium heat.

Add the chopped spinach to the skillet and sauté for 1-2 minutes, or until wilted. Remove the spinach from the skillet and set it aside.

Pour the whisked eggs into the same skillet and cook over medium-low heat. Let the eggs set for about 1-2 minutes without stirring, allowing the edges to firm up.

Add the Spinach and Feta:

Once the eggs are mostly set but still slightly runny on top, evenly distribute the cooked spinach and crumbled feta cheese over one half of the omelet.

Gently fold the other half of the omelet over the filling, covering the spinach and feta.

Cook for an additional 1-2 minutes, or until the cheese is slightly melted and the eggs are fully set.

Slide the omelet onto a plate and enjoy it while hot.

Nutritional Information per serving: *Calories: 260; Protein: 15g; Fiber: 2g; Calcium: 230mg; Magnesium: 45mg; Vit B6: 0.3mg; Vit B9: 65mcg; Vit B12: 0.9mcg; Vit C: 9mg; Vit D: 140 IU; Omega-3: 0.3g*

Tofu Scramble with Bell Peppers

Servings: 2

1 cup firm tofu, crumbled

½ cup red bell pepper, diced

½ cup spinach, chopped

1 tbsp nutritional yeast

¼ tsp turmeric

1 tsp olive oil

Crumble the tofu with your hands or a fork to resemble scrambled eggs. Dice the bell pepper and chop the spinach.

In a non-stick skillet, heat the olive oil over medium heat.

Add the diced bell pepper to the skillet and cook for 3-4 minutes until it softens.

Stir in the crumbled tofu, chopped spinach, turmeric, and nutritional yeast. Cook for an additional 5 minutes, stirring occasionally.

Add salt and pepper to taste, if desired.

Plate the scramble and enjoy it hot.

Nutritional Information per serving: *Calories: 190; Protein: 12g; Fiber: 4g; Calcium: 200mg; Magnesium: 60mg; Vit B6: 0.3mg; Vit B9: 40mcg; Vit B12: 1.5mcg; Vit C: 45mg; Vit D: 0 IU; Omega-3: 0.1g*

LUNCH RECIPES

Avocado and Sardine Salad

Baked Falafel with Tahini Sauce

Balsamic Glazed Chicken with Brussels Sprouts

Buckwheat Salad with Roasted Beets and Feta

Butternut Squash and Lentil Stew

Butternut Squash Soup with Hemp Seeds

Chickpea and Kale Stew

Chickpea Avocado Wrap

Coconut Curry Shrimp

Couscous Salad with Roasted Vegetables and Sunflower Seeds

Edamame and Avocado Salad

Garlic Herb Chicken with Roasted Vegetables

Honey Mustard Chicken Stir-Fry

Lemon Garlic Chicken with Asparagus

Lentil and Spinach Curry

Mediterranean Stuffed Bell Peppers

Miso Soup with Seaweed and Tofu

Quinoa Chickpea Salad with Lemon-Tahini Dressing

Salmon and Sweet Potato Bowl

Spicy Chickpea and Kale Stir-Fry

Spicy Coconut Chicken Curry

Sweet Potato Black Bean Tacos

Tempeh and Broccoli Stir-Fry

Tofu Kale Salad with Orange Dressing

Zucchini Noodles with Pesto and Chickpeas

Avocado and Sardine Salad

Servings: 2

1 can sardines (in water), drained

1 avocado, diced

¼ cup red onion, diced

1 cup mixed greens

1 tbsp olive oil

1 tbsp lemon juice

Salt and pepper to taste

Prepare the ingredients: Drain the sardines, dice the avocado, and chop the red onion.

Combine ingredients: In a bowl, mix the sardines, avocado, red onion, and 1 cup mixed greens.

Dress the salad: Drizzle with 1 tbsp olive oil and 1 tbsp lemon juice.

Toss and serve: Season with salt and pepper, gently toss, and serve immediately.

Nutritional Information per serving: *Calories: 320; Protein: 16g; Fiber: 7g; Calcium: 150mg; Magnesium: 70mg; Vit B6: 0.3mg; Vit B9 (Folate): 60mcg; Vit B12: 8mcg; Vit C: 10mg; Vit D: 400 IU; Omega-3 fatty acids: 2.5g*

Baked Falafel with Tahini Sauce

Servings: 4

1 can (15 oz) chickpeas, drained and rinsed

¼ cup fresh parsley, chopped

¼ cup fresh cilantro, chopped

2 cloves garlic, minced

¼ cup onion, finely chopped

2 tbsp whole-wheat flour

1 tbsp ground flaxseed (for omega-3)

1 tsp cumin

2 tbsp olive oil (divided)

Salt and pepper to taste

For the Tahini Sauce:

2 tbsp tahini

Juice of 1 lemon

1 tbsp water

Preheat the oven to 375°F (190°C). Line a baking sheet with parchment paper.

In a food processor, combine the chickpeas, parsley, cilantro, garlic, onion, flour, flaxseed, cumin, salt, and pepper. Pulse until the mixture is well combined but still slightly chunky.

Form the mixture into small balls or patties (about 2 inches in diameter).

Place the falafel on the prepared baking sheet and brush the tops with 1 tbsp olive oil.

Bake for 20-25 minutes, flipping halfway through, until golden brown.

In a small bowl, whisk together the tahini, lemon juice, and water until smooth.

Drizzle the tahini sauce over the baked falafel and serve with a side salad or pita bread.

Nutritional Information per serving: *Calories: 280; Protein: 8g; Carbohydrates: 23g; Fiber: 7g; Fat: 18g; Calcium: 70mg; Magnesium: 40mg; Vit B6: 0.2mg; Vit B9 (Folate): 130mcg; Vit B12: 0mcg; Vit C: 10mg; Vit D: 0mcg; Omega-3 Fatty Acids: 0.5g*

Balsamic Glazed Chicken with Brussels Sprouts

Servings: 4

4 boneless, skinless chicken breasts

2 cups Brussels sprouts, halved

¼ cup balsamic vinegar

2 tbsp olive oil, divided

1 tbsp honey

2 cloves garlic, minced

Salt and pepper to taste

Preheat the oven to 375°F (190°C).

In a small bowl, whisk together the balsamic vinegar, honey, and minced garlic.

Heat 1 tbsp olive oil in an oven-safe skillet over medium-high heat.

Season the chicken breasts with salt and pepper and add them to the skillet. Cook for 4-5 minutes on each side, until browned.

Add the Brussels sprouts to the skillet and drizzle with the remaining 1 tbsp olive oil.

Stir to coat everything evenly.

Roast in the oven for 15-20 minutes, until the chicken reaches an internal temperature of 165°F (74°C) and the Brussels sprouts are tender.

Divide the chicken and Brussels sprouts into four servings.

Nutritional Information per serving: *Calories: 350; Protein: 27g; Carbohydrates: 16g; Fiber: 5g; Fat: 18g; Calcium: 55mg; Magnesium: 40mg; Vit B6: 0.5mg; Vit B9 (Folate): 90mcg; Vit B12: 0.3mcg; Vit C: 60mg; Vit D: 0mcg*

Buckwheat Salad with Roasted Beets and Feta

Servings: 4

1 cup cooked buckwheat

2 roasted beets, diced

¼ cup crumbled feta cheese

¼ cup walnuts, chopped (for omega-3)

1 tbsp ground flaxseed

1 tbsp olive oil

1 tbsp apple cider vinegar

Salt and pepper to taste

Prepare 1 cup of buckwheat according to package instructions. Let it cool.

Preheat the oven to 375°F (190°C). Wrap the beets in foil and roast for 45-60 minutes, until tender. Let them cool, then peel and dice.

In a large bowl, combine the cooked buckwheat, diced roasted beets, ¼ cup crumbled feta cheese, ¼ cup chopped walnuts, and 1 tbsp ground flaxseed.

Drizzle with 1 tbsp olive oil and 1 tbsp apple cider vinegar. Season with salt and pepper.

Mix the ingredients thoroughly before serving.

Nutritional Information per serving: *Calories: 290; Protein: 8g; Fiber: 7g; Calcium: 130mg; Magnesium: 60mg; Vit B6: 0.2mg; Vit B9 (Folate): 80mcg; Vit B12: 0.4mcg; Vit C: 15mg; Vit D: 0 IU; Omega-3 fatty acids: 1.5g*

Butternut Squash and Lentil Stew

Servings: 4

1 medium butternut squash, peeled and cubed

1 cup red lentils, rinsed

1 onion, chopped

2 cloves garlic, minced

1 tbsp olive oil

1 tsp cumin

1 tsp turmeric

4 cups vegetable broth

2 cups spinach, chopped

1 tbsp ground flaxseed (for omega-3)

Salt and pepper to taste

In a large pot, heat the olive oil over medium heat.

Add the chopped onion and cook for 5 minutes, until soft.

Stir in the minced garlic, cumin, and turmeric, cooking for an additional minute.

Add the cubed butternut squash, red lentils, and vegetable broth.

Bring to boil, then reduce heat and simmer for 25-30 minutes, until the squash is tender and the lentils are cooked.

Stir in the chopped spinach and ground flaxseed.

Cook for another 5 minutes, until the spinach is wilted.

Season with salt and pepper to taste before serving.

Nutritional Information per serving: *Calories: 300;
Protein: 14g; Carbohydrates: 48g; Fiber: 12g; Fat: 7g;
Calcium: 80mg; Magnesium: 70mg; Vit B6: 0.4mg; Vit B9
(Folate): 180mcg; Vit B12: 0mcg; Vit C: 30mg; Vit D:
0mcg; Omega-3 Fatty Acids: 0.6g*

Butternut Squash Soup with Hemp Seeds

Servings: 4

1 medium butternut squash, peeled and cubed

1 medium onion, chopped

2 cloves garlic, minced

1 tbsp olive oil

4 cups vegetable broth

¼ cup hemp seeds (for omega-3)

½ cup coconut milk

½ tsp nutmeg

Salt and pepper to taste

Peel and cube the butternut squash, chop the onion, and mince the garlic.

Heat 1 tbsp olive oil in a large pot over medium heat. Add the chopped onion and minced garlic, cooking for 3-4 minutes until soft.

Add the cubed butternut squash and 4 cups of vegetable broth to the pot. Bring to a boil, then reduce the heat and simmer for 20 minutes, or until the squash is tender.

Stir in ¼ cup hemp seeds, ½ cup coconut milk, and ½ tsp nutmeg. Use an immersion blender to blend the soup until smooth.

Add salt and pepper to taste. Serve the soup warm.

Nutritional Information per serving: *Calories: 230; Protein: 6g; Fiber: 5g; Calcium: 80mg; Magnesium: 70mg; Vit B6: 0.4mg; Vit B9 (Folate): 50mcg; Vit B12: 0mcg; Vit C: 20mg; Vit D: 0 IU; Omega-3 fatty acids: 2.5g*

Chickpea and Kale Stew

Servings: 4

1 can (15 oz) chickpeas, drained and rinsed

2 cups kale, chopped

1 medium potato, diced

½ cup coconut milk

1 tbsp olive oil

1 onion, chopped

2 cloves garlic, minced

1 tsp cumin

1 tsp paprika

Salt and pepper

Drain and rinse the chickpeas, chop the kale, and dice the potato.

Heat 1 tbsp olive oil in a large pot over medium heat. Add the chopped onion and minced garlic, cooking for 3-4 minutes until soft.

Stir in the diced potato, chickpeas, 1 tsp cumin, and 1 tsp paprika. Cook for 10 minutes, stirring occasionally.

Add the chopped kale and ½ cup coconut milk. Simmer for another 10 minutes, until the kale is tender, and the stew is heated through.

Add salt and pepper to taste before serving.

Nutritional Information per serving: *Calories: 260; Protein: 9g; Fiber: 8g; Calcium: 110mg; Magnesium: 70mg; Vit B6: 0.3mg; Vit B9 (Folate): 80mcg; Vit B12: 0mcg; Vit C: 25mg; Vit D: 0 IU; Omega-3 fatty acids: 1g*

Chickpea Avocado Wrap

Servings: 2

1 ripe avocado, mashed

1 cup chickpeas, mashed

¼ cup red onion, diced

1 tbsp chia seeds

1 tbsp lemon juice

½ cup shredded lettuce

1 medium tomato, sliced

2 whole-grain tortillas

Salt and pepper to taste

If using canned chickpeas, drain and rinse them thoroughly. If using cooked chickpeas, ensure they are cooled.

In a medium bowl, mash the chickpeas using a fork or potato masher until they are mostly smooth, with some chunks remaining for texture.

Cut the avocado in half, remove the pit, and scoop the flesh into the bowl with the mashed chickpeas. Mash the avocado thoroughly and mix it with the chickpeas.

Add the diced red onion, chia seeds, and lemon juice to the chickpea and avocado mixture.

Season with salt and pepper to taste, and stir everything together until well combined.

Lay the whole-grain tortillas flat on a clean surface.

Divide the chickpea-avocado mixture evenly between the two tortillas, spreading it over the center of each tortilla, leaving about an inch around the edges.

Add an even layer of shredded lettuce over the chickpea-avocado mixture, then place the tomato slices on top.

Fold the sides of each tortilla inward, then roll from the bottom up to form a wrap, enclosing the filling securely.

For a firmer wrap, you can toast the assembled wraps in a skillet over medium heat for 1-2 minutes on each side (optional).

Nutritional Information per serving: *Calories: 340; Protein: 9g; Fiber: 12g; Calcium: 60mg; Magnesium: 70mg; Vit B6: 0.4mg; Vit B9 (Folate): 130mcg; Vit B12: 0mcg; Vit C: 15mg; Vit D: 0 IU; Omega-3 fatty acids: 1.5g*

Coconut Curry Shrimp

Servings: 4

1 lb large shrimp, peeled and deveined

1 tbsp olive oil

1 small onion, diced

2 cloves garlic, minced

1 tbsp fresh ginger, minced

1 cup coconut milk

2 tbsp red curry paste

1 bell pepper, thinly sliced

1 cup spinach, chopped

1 tbsp lime juice

Salt and pepper to taste

Fresh cilantro for garnish

Season the shrimp with salt and pepper and set aside.

Heat the olive oil in a skillet over medium heat. Add the onion, garlic, and ginger, cooking for 3-4 minutes until softened.

Stir in the red curry paste and cook for 1 minute. Add the coconut milk, stirring until the mixture is well-combined.

Add the bell pepper and spinach to the skillet. Cook for 2-3 minutes until the vegetables start to soften.

Add the shrimp to the skillet and cook for 5-6 minutes, or until they are pink and cooked through.

Stir in the lime juice and sprinkle with fresh cilantro before serving.

Pair with rice or quinoa for a complete meal.

Nutritional Information per serving: *Calories: 280, Protein: 24g, Carbohydrates: 8g, Fiber: 2g, Fat: 18g, Calcium: 80mg, Magnesium: 50mg, Vit B6: 0.3mg, Vit B9 (Folate): 35mcg, Vit B12: 1.3mcg, Vit C: 30mg, Vit D: 0.2mcg, Omega-3 Fatty Acids: 0.4g*

Couscous Salad with Roasted Vegetables and Sunflower Seeds

Servings: 4

1 cup whole wheat couscous

2 cups mixed vegetables (zucchini, bell peppers, carrots), roasted

¼ cup sunflower seeds

1 tbsp ground flaxseed (for omega-3)

2 tbsp olive oil

1 tbsp balsamic vinegar

Salt and pepper to taste

Cook 1 cup of whole wheat couscous according to package instructions. Fluff with a fork and set aside.

Roast 2 cups of mixed vegetables (zucchini, bell peppers, carrots) at 375°F (190°C) for 20-25 minutes, until tender.

In a large bowl, mix the cooked couscous, roasted vegetables, ¼ cup sunflower seeds, and 1 tbsp ground flaxseed.

Drizzle with 2 tbsp olive oil and 1 tbsp balsamic vinegar. Season with salt and pepper to taste.

Toss to combine and serve warm or at room temperature.

Nutritional Information per serving: *Calories: 280; Protein: 8g; Fiber: 6g; Calcium: 40mg; Magnesium: 60mg; Vit B6: 0.2mg; Vit B9 (Folate): 50mcg; Vit B12: 0mcg; Vit C: 15mg; Vit D: 0 IU; Omega-3 fatty acids: 1g*

Edamame and Avocado Salad

Servings: 4

1 cup shelled edamame, cooked

1 avocado, diced

1 cup cherry tomatoes, halved

¼ cup red onion, chopped

2 tbsp chia seeds (for omega-3)

1 tbsp olive oil

Juice of 1 lime

Salt and pepper to taste

Cook the shelled edamame according to package instructions, then let it cool. Dice the avocado, halve the cherry tomatoes, and chop the red onion.

In a large bowl, combine 1 cup edamame, diced avocado, cherry tomatoes, red onion, and 2 tbsp chia seeds.

Drizzle 1 tbsp olive oil and the juice of 1 lime over the salad. Season with salt and pepper.

Gently toss the ingredients to coat them in the dressing. Serve immediately.

Nutritional Information per serving: *Calories: 250; Protein: 8g; Fiber: 8g; Calcium: 60mg; Magnesium: 60mg; Vit B6: 0.3mg; Vit B9 (Folate): 90mcg; Vit B12: 0mcg; Vit C: 20mg; Vit D: 0 IU; Omega-3 fatty acids: 2g*

Garlic Herb Chicken with Roasted Vegetables

Servings: 4

4 boneless, skinless chicken breasts (about 5-6 oz each)

2 tbsp olive oil, divided

3 cloves garlic, minced

1 tsp dried oregano

1 tsp dried thyme

½ tsp dried rosemary

Salt and pepper to taste

2 cups broccoli florets

2 medium carrots, sliced

1 red onion, cut into wedges

1 lemon, sliced

Preheat the oven to 400°F (200°C).

In a small bowl, mix the minced garlic, oregano, thyme, rosemary, salt, and pepper with 1 tbsp olive oil.

Rub the mixture evenly over the chicken breasts.

On a baking sheet, toss the broccoli, carrots, and red onion with the remaining 1 tbsp olive oil, salt, and pepper.

Spread the vegetables out in a single layer and place the seasoned chicken breasts on top.

Place lemon slices over the chicken and vegetables for added flavor.

Roast in the oven for 25-30 minutes, or until the chicken reaches an internal temperature of 165°F (74°C) and the vegetables are tender.

Divide the chicken and roasted vegetables into four servings and enjoy immediately.

Nutritional Information per serving: *Calories: 350; Protein: 34g; Carbohydrates: 12g; Fiber: 4g; Fat: 18g; Calcium: 50mg; Magnesium: 60mg; Vit B6: 0.8mg; Vit B9 (Folate): 60mcg; Vit B12: 0.3mcg; Vit C: 40mg; Vit D: 0mcg*

Honey Mustard Chicken Stir-Fry

Servings: 4

4 boneless, skinless chicken breasts, sliced

2 tbsp honey

2 tbsp Dijon mustard

2 tbsp olive oil, divided

1 red bell pepper, sliced

1 yellow bell pepper, sliced

1 small onion, sliced

2 cups snap peas

2 cloves garlic, minced

Salt and pepper to taste

In a small bowl, whisk together the honey and Dijon mustard. Set aside.

Heat 1 tbsp olive oil in a large skillet over medium-high heat.

Add the sliced chicken breasts and cook for 5-7 minutes, until browned and cooked through. Remove from the skillet and set aside.

In the same skillet, add the remaining 1 tbsp olive oil.

Add the sliced bell peppers, onion, snap peas, and garlic. Cook for 5-6 minutes, stirring frequently, until the vegetables are tender-crisp.

Return the cooked chicken to the skillet.

Pour the honey mustard sauce over the chicken and vegetables, stirring to coat everything evenly.

Cook for an additional 2-3 minutes, until heated through.

Divide the stir-fry into four servings. It can be enjoyed on its own or served over brown rice or quinoa.

Nutritional Information per serving: *Calories: 320; Protein: 28g; Carbohydrates: 18g; Fiber: 3g; Fat: 16g; Calcium: 40mg; Magnesium: 45mg; Vit B6: 0.7mg; Vit B9 (Folate): 50mcg; Vit B12: 0.2mcg; Vit C: 60mg; Vit D: 0mcg*

Lemon Garlic Chicken with Asparagus

Servings: 4

4 boneless, skinless chicken breasts

1 bunch asparagus, trimmed

2 tbsp olive oil, divided

3 cloves garlic, minced

Juice of 1 lemon

¼ cup chicken broth

Salt and pepper to taste

½ tsp red pepper flakes (optional)

Season the chicken breasts with salt and pepper.

Heat 1 tbsp olive oil in a skillet over medium-high heat.

Add the chicken breasts and cook for 5-7 minutes on each side, until golden brown and cooked through.

Remove the chicken from the skillet and set aside.

In the same skillet, add the remaining 1 tbsp olive oil and garlic. Cook for 1 minute, stirring frequently.

Add the asparagus and cook for 4-5 minutes, until tender-crisp.

Add the lemon juice and chicken broth:

Pour in the lemon juice and chicken broth. Stir to combine.

Return the chicken to the skillet and cook for an additional 2-3 minutes, until the sauce has thickened slightly.

Divide the chicken and asparagus into four servings and drizzle with the lemon-garlic sauce.

Nutritional Information per serving: Calories: 280; Protein: 33g; Carbohydrates: 7g; Fiber: 3g; Fat: 14g; Calcium: 50mg; Magnesium: 50mg; Vit B6: 0.9mg; Vit B9 (Folate): 70mcg; Vit B12: 0.3mcg; Vit C: 15mg; Vit D: 0mcg

Lentil and Spinach Curry

Servings: 4

1 cup red lentils, rinsed

2 cups fresh spinach, chopped

½ cup coconut milk

1 medium onion, chopped

2 cloves garlic, minced

1 tbsp curry powder

1 tsp turmeric

1 tbsp olive oil

1 cup vegetable broth

1 tbsp ground flaxseed (for omega-3)

Salt and pepper to taste

Rinse the red lentils thoroughly under cold water and set them aside.

Chop the onion and mince the garlic.

In a large pot, heat the olive oil over medium heat.

Add the chopped onion and cook for about 5 minutes, stirring occasionally, until the onion is soft and translucent.

Add the minced garlic and cook for an additional 1-2 minutes, until fragrant.

Stir in the curry powder and turmeric, cooking for 1 minute to toast the spices and bring out their flavors.

Add the rinsed red lentils to the pot, along with the vegetable broth.

Stir well, bring the mixture to a boil, then reduce the heat to a simmer.

Cover the pot and let the lentils simmer for about 15-20 minutes, stirring occasionally, until they are tender and have absorbed most of the liquid.

Stir in the coconut milk and chopped spinach.

Simmer for an additional 5 minutes, until the spinach is wilted and the curry is heated through.

Stir in the ground flaxseed, and season the curry with salt and pepper to taste.

Remove the pot from the heat and let the curry rest for a couple of minutes.

Serve the lentil and spinach curry over rice or with naan bread, if desired.

Nutritional Information per serving: *Calories: 250; Protein: 12g; Fiber: 9g; Calcium: 80mg; Magnesium: 60mg; Vit B6: 0.3mg; Vit B9 (Folate): 150mcg; Vit B12: 0mcg; Vit C: 10mg; Vit D: 0 IU; Omega-3 fatty acids: 1g*

Mediterranean Stuffed Bell Peppers

Servings: 4

4 bell peppers, halved and seeded

1 cup cooked brown rice

1 can (15 oz) white beans, drained and rinsed

½ cup cherry tomatoes, diced

¼ cup Kalamata olives, sliced

2 tbsp ground flaxseed (for omega-3)

¼ cup feta cheese

1 tbsp olive oil

1 tsp oregano

Preheat the oven to 375°F (190°C). Line a baking dish with parchment paper or lightly grease it with olive oil.

Place the halved and seeded bell peppers in the baking dish, cut side up. Drizzle them lightly with olive oil and sprinkle with a little salt and pepper.

In a large bowl, combine the cooked brown rice, white beans, diced cherry tomatoes, sliced Kalamata olives, ground flaxseed, oregano, and a pinch of salt and pepper. Mix well to ensure all ingredients are evenly distributed.

Spoon the rice and bean mixture evenly into each of the bell pepper halves, pressing down gently to pack the filling. Sprinkle the tops with crumbled feta cheese.

Cover the baking dish with aluminum foil and bake in the preheated oven for 30 minutes. Then, remove the foil and bake for an additional 10-15 minutes, or until the peppers are tender and the filling is heated through.

Remove the stuffed peppers from the oven and let them cool for a few minutes before serving. Drizzle with a bit more olive oil if desired.

Nutritional Information per serving: *Calories: 330; Protein: 11g; Fiber: 8g; Calcium: 120mg; Magnesium: 70mg; Vit B6: 0.3mg; Vit B9 (Folate): 80mcg; Vit B12: 0.3mcg; Vit C: 60mg; Vit D: 0 IU; Omega-3 fatty acids: 1g*

Miso Soup with Seaweed and Tofu

Servings: 4

4 cups vegetable broth

1 block tofu, cubed

2 tbsp miso paste

¼ cup seaweed, soaked

2 green onions, chopped

1 tbsp ground flaxseed (for omega-3)

1 tsp soy sauce

In a large pot, bring 4 cups of vegetable broth to a gentle boil.

Add the cubed tofu and soaked seaweed. Simmer for 5 minutes.

In a small bowl, mix 2 tbsp miso paste with a little hot broth until smooth. Stir the mixture back into the soup.

Stir in 1 tsp soy sauce, 1 tbsp ground flaxseed, and chopped green onions.

Ladle the soup into bowls and serve hot.

Nutritional Information per serving: *Calories: 170; Protein: 8g; Fiber: 2g; Calcium: 140mg; Magnesium: 50mg; Vit B6: 0.1mg; Vit B9 (Folate): 30mcg; Vit B12: 0.1mcg; Vit C: 5mg; Vit D: 0 IU; Omega-3 fatty acids: 1g*

Quinoa Chickpea Salad with Lemon-Tahini Dressing

Servings: 4

1 cup quinoa, cooked

1 can (15 oz) chickpeas, drained and rinsed

1 cup cherry tomatoes, halved

1 cup cucumber, diced

¼ cup red onion, finely chopped

2 tbsp chia seeds (for omega-3)

¼ cup feta cheese (for calcium and Vit B12)

¼ cup fresh parsley, chopped

Juice of 1 lemon (for Vit C)

2 tbsp tahini

1 tbsp olive oil

Salt and pepper to taste

If not already cooked, prepare 1 cup of quinoa according to package instructions. Use 2 cups of water for every 1 cup of quinoa.

Bring the water to a boil, add the quinoa, reduce the heat to a simmer, and cover. Cook for 15 minutes or until the water is absorbed and the quinoa is fluffy.

Let the quinoa cool completely before using it in the salad.

While the quinoa is cooling, drain and rinse the chickpeas thoroughly.

Halve the cherry tomatoes, dice the cucumber, and finely chop the red onion.

Chop the fresh parsley and set aside.

Make the lemon-tahini dressing:

In a small bowl, whisk together the lemon juice, tahini, and olive oil.

Season with salt and pepper to taste. If the dressing is too thick, add a small amount of water (1-2 tsp) to reach the desired consistency.

In a large mixing bowl, combine the cooked quinoa, chickpeas, cherry tomatoes, cucumber, red onion, chia seeds, and chopped parsley.

Drizzle the lemon-tahini dressing over the salad and toss well to coat all the ingredients.

Gently fold in the feta cheese, making sure it is evenly distributed throughout the salad.

Season with additional salt and pepper if needed.

Divide the salad into four servings and enjoy immediately.

This salad can also be stored in the refrigerator for up to 2 days, making it great for meal prep.

Nutritional Information per serving: *Calories: 300; Protein: 10g; Fiber: 7g; Calcium: 150mg; Magnesium: 90mg; Vit B6: 0.4mg; Vit B9 (Folate): 90mcg; Vit B12: 0.6mcg; Vit C: 20mg; Vit D: 0 IU; Omega-3 fatty acids: 1.5g*

Salmon and Sweet Potato Bowl

Servings: 4

2 medium sweet potatoes, peeled and diced

4 salmon fillets (4 oz each)

4 cups baby spinach

1 avocado, sliced

1 tbsp olive oil

2 tbsp ground flaxseed (for omega-3)

¼ cup chopped walnuts (for omega-3)

Salt and pepper to taste

1 lemon, sliced (for serving)

Preheat the oven to 400°F (200°C). Line a baking sheet with parchment paper or lightly grease it.

Roast the sweet potatoes: Place the diced sweet potatoes on the prepared baking sheet. Drizzle with 1 tbsp olive oil, and season with salt and pepper. Toss to coat. Roast in the preheated oven for 20 minutes.

Add the salmon: While the sweet potatoes are roasting, season the salmon fillets with salt and pepper. Add them to the baking sheet with the sweet potatoes after 20 minutes. Continue roasting for another 15 minutes or until the salmon is cooked through and flakes easily with a fork.

Assemble the bowls: Divide the roasted sweet potatoes and salmon among four bowls. Add 1 cup of spinach, a few avocado slices, 1 tbsp walnuts, and 1/2 tbsp flaxseed to each bowl.

Serve: Squeeze fresh lemon juice over each bowl just before serving.

Nutritional Information per serving: *Calories: 450; Protein: 30g; Fiber: 9g; Calcium: 80mg; Magnesium: 90mg; Vit B6: 0.7mg; Vit B9 (Folate): 90mcg; Vit B12: 4mcg; Vit C: 30mg; Vit D: 600 IU; Omega-3 fatty acids: 3.5g*

Spicy Chickpea and Kale Stir-Fry

Servings: 4

1 can (15 oz) chickpeas, drained and rinsed

4 cups kale, chopped

1 red bell pepper, thinly sliced

1 small onion, thinly sliced

2 cloves garlic, minced

2 tbsp olive oil

1 tbsp soy sauce (or tamari for gluten-free)

1 tbsp hot sauce (optional, for spice)

1 tbsp ground flaxseed (for omega-3)

1 tsp smoked paprika

¼ tsp red pepper flakes (optional, for extra spice)

Salt and pepper to taste

Juice of ½ lemon

Drain and rinse the chickpeas thoroughly.

Chop the kale and thinly slice the red bell pepper and onion. Mince the garlic.

Heat the olive oil in a large skillet over medium heat.

Add the sliced onion and cook for about 3-4 minutes, stirring frequently, until softened.

Add the minced garlic, red bell pepper, and smoked paprika, and cook for another 2-3 minutes, until the peppers start to soften.

Stir in the chickpeas, chopped kale, soy sauce, and hot sauce (if using).

Cook for 5-7 minutes, stirring occasionally, until the kale is wilted, and the chickpeas are heated through.

Add the ground flaxseed, lemon juice, and red pepper flakes (if using).

Season with salt and pepper to taste. Stir everything together for an additional minute.

Divide the stir-fry into four servings. It can be enjoyed on its own or served over a bed of rice or quinoa.

Nutritional Information per serving: *Calories: 240; Protein: 8g; Carbohydrates: 26g; Fiber: 8g; Fat: 12g; Calcium: 110mg; Magnesium: 50mg; Vit B6: 0.3mg; Vit B9 (Folate): 40mcg; Vit B12: 0mcg; Vit C: 60mg; Vit D: 0mcg; Omega-3 Fatty Acids: 0.6g*

Spicy Coconut Chicken Curry

Servings: 4

4 boneless, skinless chicken breasts, cubed

1 can (13.5 oz) coconut milk

2 tbsp olive oil

1 onion, diced

2 cloves garlic, minced

1 tbsp curry powder

1 tsp turmeric

½ tsp cayenne pepper (optional, for spice)

1 can (15 oz) diced tomatoes

2 cups spinach, chopped

Salt and pepper to taste

Cook the onion and garlic:

Heat the olive oil in a large pot over medium heat.

Add the diced onion and cook for 5 minutes, until softened.

Stir in the minced garlic, curry powder, turmeric, and cayenne pepper, and cook for another 1-2 minutes.

Add the cubed chicken to the pot and cook for 5-7 minutes, stirring frequently, until the chicken is browned on all sides.

Pour in the coconut milk and diced tomatoes (including the juice). Stir to combine.

Bring the mixture to a simmer and cook for 15-20 minutes, until the chicken is cooked through and the sauce has thickened.

Stir in the chopped spinach and cook for an additional 2-3 minutes, until wilted.

Divide the curry into four servings. It can be enjoyed on its own or served over brown rice or quinoa.

Nutritional Information per serving: *Calories: 400; Protein: 33g; Carbohydrates: 12g; Fiber: 4g; Fat: 24g; Calcium: 60mg; Magnesium: 55mg; Vit B6: 0.8mg; Vit B9 (Folate): 80mcg; Vit B12: 0.2mcg; Vit C: 20mg; Vit D: 0mcg*

Sweet Potato Black Bean Tacos

Servings: 4

2 medium sweet potatoes, peeled and diced

1 can (15 oz) black beans, drained and rinsed

1 small red onion, finely chopped

1 red bell pepper, diced

2 tbsp olive oil, divided

1 tsp cumin

½ tsp smoked paprika

½ tsp chili powder

Salt and pepper to taste

8 small corn tortillas

¼ cup fresh cilantro, chopped

1 avocado, sliced (optional)

¼ cup crumbled feta cheese (optional)

Lime wedges for serving

Preheat the oven to 400°F (200°C). Line a baking sheet with parchment paper.

Place the diced sweet potatoes on the prepared baking sheet and drizzle with 1 tbsp olive oil.

Sprinkle with cumin, smoked paprika, chili powder, salt, and pepper. Toss to coat evenly.

Roast for 25-30 minutes, turning halfway through, until the sweet potatoes are tender and slightly crispy.

In a skillet, heat the remaining 1 tbsp of olive oil over medium heat.

Add the chopped red onion and red bell pepper. Cook for 5-7 minutes, stirring occasionally, until they are softened.

Add the black beans and cook for an additional 3-4 minutes, until heated through.

Warm the corn tortillas in a dry skillet or microwave.

Divide the roasted sweet potatoes and black bean mixture evenly among the tortillas.

Top with chopped cilantro, avocado slices, and feta cheese, if using.

Serve with lime wedges on the side.

Nutritional Information per serving: *Calories: 320; Protein: 9g; Carbohydrates: 46g; Fiber: 10g; Fat: 11g; Calcium: 90mg; Magnesium: 60mg; Vit B6: 0.4mg; Vit B9 (Folate): 140mcg; Vit B12: 0.5mcg (with feta); Vit C: 30mg; Vit D: 0mcg; Omega-3 Fatty Acids: 0.2g*

Tempeh and Broccoli Stir-Fry

Servings: 4

1 block tempeh, cubed

3 cups broccoli florets

1 red bell pepper, sliced

2 tbsp chia seeds (for omega-3)

1 tbsp olive oil

2 tbsp soy sauce

1 tbsp rice vinegar

2 cloves garlic, minced

1 tsp ginger, minced

Cube the tempeh, chop the broccoli florets, and slice the bell pepper.

Heat 1 tbsp olive oil in a large skillet or wok over medium heat. Add the cubed tempeh and cook for 4-5 minutes, stirring occasionally, until browned on all sides.

Stir in the minced garlic and ginger, cooking for an additional minute until fragrant.

Add the broccoli florets and bell pepper slices. Stir-fry for 5-7 minutes, until the vegetables are tender-crisp.

Stir in the soy sauce, rice vinegar, and chia seeds. Cook for 1-2 minutes to let the flavors combine.

Serve immediately, garnished with additional chia seeds if desired.

Nutritional Information per serving: *Calories: 320; Protein: 16g; Fiber: 8g; Calcium: 150mg; Magnesium: 70mg; Vit B6: 0.5mg; Vit B9 (Folate): 90mcg; Vit B12: 0mcg; Vit C: 80mg; Vit D: 0 IU; Omega-3 fatty acids: 2g*

Tofu Kale Salad with Orange Dressing

Servings: 4

1 block firm tofu, cubed

4 cups kale, chopped

1 orange, juiced

¼ cup walnuts, chopped (for omega-3)

2 tbsp olive oil

½ cup red bell pepper, diced

¼ cup sunflower seeds

¼ cup feta cheese (optional)

Salt and pepper to taste

Drain the tofu and press it to remove excess moisture. Place it between paper towels or a clean kitchen towel, and gently press down with a heavy object for 10-15 minutes.

Cut the tofu into small cubes once it is well-drained.

Heat 1 tbsp of olive oil in a skillet over medium-high heat.

Add the cubed tofu to the skillet and season with salt and pepper.

Cook for 6-8 minutes, turning occasionally, until the tofu is golden brown and slightly crispy on all sides.

Remove from heat and set aside to cool.

Place the chopped kale in a large bowl.

Massage the kale by gently squeezing and rubbing the leaves for about 2-3 minutes. This helps to soften the kale and reduce its bitterness.

In a small bowl, whisk together the fresh orange juice and the remaining 1 tbsp of olive oil.

Add a pinch of salt and pepper and mix well.

Add the cooked tofu, diced red bell pepper, chopped walnuts, and sunflower seeds to the massaged kale.

Pour the orange dressing over the salad and toss well to combine.

If using, sprinkle the feta cheese on top of the salad.

Divide the salad into four servings and enjoy immediately.

Nutritional Information per serving: *Calories: 290; Protein: 13g; Fiber: 6g; Calcium: 180mg; Magnesium: 80mg; Vit B6: 0.4mg; Vit B9 (Folate): 110mcg; Vit B12: 0.3mcg; Vit C: 40mg; Vit D: 0 IU; Omega-3 fatty acids: 2g*

Zucchini Noodles with Pesto and Chickpeas

Servings: 4

4 medium zucchini, spiralized into noodles

1 cup fresh basil leaves

¼ cup walnuts (for omega-3)

¼ cup Parmesan cheese, grated

1 clove garlic

¼ cup olive oil

1 can (15 oz) chickpeas, drained and rinsed

½ cup cherry tomatoes, halved

Salt and pepper to taste

In a food processor, combine the basil leaves, walnuts, Parmesan cheese, garlic, and a pinch of salt and pepper.

While the processor is running, gradually add the olive oil until a smooth paste forms. Set aside.

In a large skillet, heat a small amount of olive oil over medium heat.

Add the spiralized zucchini noodles and cook for 3-4 minutes, stirring frequently, until they are slightly softened but not mushy.

Add the chickpeas and cherry tomatoes to the skillet with the zucchini noodles.

Stir in the pesto and toss to coat everything evenly.

Divide the zucchini noodles among four plates.

Top with additional Parmesan cheese if desired.

Nutritional Information per serving: Calories: 350; Protein: 10g; Carbohydrates: 23g; Fiber: 6g; Fat: 26g; Calcium: 130mg; Magnesium: 70mg; Vit B6: 0.3mg; Vit B9 (Folate): 120mcg; Vit B12: 0.2mcg (with Parmesan); Vit C: 25mg; Vit D: 0mcg; Omega-3 Fatty Acids: 0.5g

DINNER RECIPES

Baked Chicken Parmesan

Baked Lemon Herb Salmon

Baked Salmon with Asparagus

Baked Tofu and Broccoli

Chicken and Vegetable Stir-Fry

Chickpea and Vegetable Casserole

Chickpea and Stir-Fry

Chili Lime Mahi Mahi

Cilantro Lime Rice Bowl

Garlic Butter Tilapia

Greek Quinoa Bowl

Lentil Soup Extravaganza

Meatless Stuffed Bell Peppers

Mediterranean Baked Cod

Mushroom and Spinach Risotto

Pan-Seared Trout with Almonds

Pistachio-Crusted Salmon

Quinoa and Black Bean Salad

Roasted Chickpeas and Sweet Potatoes

Spicy Tuna Patties

Spinach and Feta Stuffed Portobello Mushrooms

Spinach and Mushroom Garlic Pasta

Teriyaki Glazed Swordfish

Vegetable and Chickpea Curry

Vegetable Pasta Primavera

Vegetable Stir-Fried Quinoa

Zucchini Noodles with Pesto

Baked Chicken Parmesan

Servings: 4

4 boneless, skinless chicken breasts

1 cup marinara sauce

1 cup shredded mozzarella cheese

½ cup grated Parmesan cheese

1 cup whole wheat breadcrumbs

1 tsp Italian seasoning

Salt and pepper to taste

Preheat your oven to 375°F (190°C).

Season the chicken breasts with salt, pepper, and Italian seasoning.

Place the breadcrumbs in a shallow dish and coat each chicken breast in the breadcrumbs.

Place the breaded chicken breasts in a baking dish.

Bake the chicken for 20 minutes, then remove from the oven and spoon marinara sauce over each piece.

Sprinkle mozzarella and Parmesan cheese on top of the marinara sauce.

Return to the oven and bake for an additional 10-15 minutes, or until the cheese is bubbly and the chicken reaches an internal temperature of 165°F (75°C).

Serve hot with a side salad or whole grain pasta.

Nutritional Information per serving: *Calories: 400, Protein: 35g, Fiber: 2g, Calcium: 300mg, Magnesium: 40mg, Vit B6: 0.6mg, Vit B9: 10mcg, Vit B12: 0.5mcg, Vit C: 5mg, Vit D: 0IU, Omega-3: 0g*

Baked Lemon Herb Salmon

Servings: 4

4 salmon fillets

2 lemons, sliced

2 tbsp olive oil

1 tbsp fresh dill, chopped

Salt and pepper to taste

Preheat your oven to 375°F (190°C).

Place the salmon fillets on a baking sheet lined with parchment paper.

Drizzle olive oil over the salmon and season with salt and pepper.

Lay lemon slices on top of each fillet and sprinkle with fresh dill.

Bake for 15-20 minutes, or until the salmon is cooked through and flakes easily with a fork.

Serve hot with a side of steamed vegetables or a fresh salad.

Nutritional Information per serving: *Calories: 320, Protein: 30g, Fiber: 0g, Calcium: 30mg, Magnesium: 50mg, Vit B6: 0.5mg, Vit B9: 10mcg, Vit B12: 4mcg, Vit C: 20mg, Vit D: 600IU, Omega-3: 1.5g*

Baked Salmon with Asparagus

Servings: 2

2 salmon fillets (4 oz each)

2 cups asparagus

2 tbsp olive oil

1 lemon, juiced

Salt and pepper to taste

Preheat your oven to 400°F (200°C).

Line a baking sheet with parchment paper for easy cleanup.

Place the salmon fillets on one side of the baking sheet and the asparagus on the other.

Drizzle olive oil and lemon juice over the salmon and asparagus.

Season with salt and pepper.

Bake for 12-15 minutes, or until the salmon is cooked through and flakes easily with a fork.

Serve immediately.

Nutritional Information per serving: *Calories: 400, Protein: 35g, Fiber: 4g, Calcium: 40mg, Magnesium: 30mg, Vit B6: 0.6mg, Vit B9: 10mcg, Vit B12: 3.5mcg, Vit C: 5mg, Vit D: 600IU, Omega-3: 2.5g*

Baked Tofu and Broccoli

Servings: 4

1 block firm tofu, pressed and cubed

2 cups broccoli florets

2 tbsp soy sauce

1 tbsp olive oil

1 tbsp sesame seeds

Preheat your oven to 400°F (200°C).

Toss the cubed tofu and broccoli in a bowl with soy sauce and olive oil.

Spread the mixture on a baking sheet and sprinkle sesame seeds over it.

Bake for 25-30 minutes until the tofu is golden and the broccoli is tender.

Serve warm over rice or quinoa.

Nutritional Information per serving: *Calories: 290, Protein: 20g, Fiber: 7g, Calcium: 250mg, Magnesium: 70mg, Vit B6: 0.2mg, Vit B9: 30mcg, Vit B12: 0mcg, Vit C: 50mg, Vit D: 0IU, Omega-3: 0.1g*

Chicken and Vegetable Stir-Fry

Servings: 4

1 lb boneless, skinless chicken breasts, sliced

2 cups mixed bell peppers, sliced

1 cup broccoli florets

2 cups snap peas

2 tbsp soy sauce

1 tbsp sesame oil

2 cloves garlic, minced

1 inch ginger, grated

1 tbsp cornstarch (optional for thickening)

Heat the sesame oil in a large skillet or wok over medium-high heat.

Add the sliced chicken breasts and cook for about 5-7 minutes until browned and cooked through.

Add the minced garlic and grated ginger, sautéing for another minute.

Add the mixed bell peppers, broccoli, and snap peas to the skillet. Stir-fry for about 5 minutes until the vegetables are tender-crisp.

In a small bowl, mix the soy sauce with cornstarch (if using) and add it to the skillet. Stir well to combine and cook for another 2 minutes until the sauce thickens.

Serve hot over brown rice or quinoa.

Nutritional Information per serving: Calories: 350, Protein: 30g, Fiber: 5g, Calcium: 60mg, Magnesium: 50mg, Vit B6: 0.5mg, Vit B9: 15mcg, Vit B12: 0.5mcg, Vit C: 70mg, Vit D: 0IU, Omega-3: 0.2g

Chickpea and Vegetable Casserole

Servings: 6

1 can chickpeas (15 oz), rinsed

2 cups mixed vegetables (carrots, peas, corn)

1 cup vegetable broth

1 cup quinoa, cooked

1 tsp Italian seasoning

Preheat your oven to 375°F (190°C).

In a mixing bowl, combine the chickpeas, mixed vegetables, cooked quinoa, vegetable broth, and Italian seasoning.

Pour the mixture into a greased baking dish.

Cover with foil and bake for 25-30 minutes.

Remove the foil for the last 10 minutes to allow it to brown slightly.

Serve hot.

Nutritional Information per serving: *Calories: 220, Protein: 10g, Fiber: 8g, Calcium: 40mg, Magnesium: 50mg, Vit B6: 0.2mg, Vit B9: 70mcg, Vit B12: 0mcg, Vit C: 30mg, Vit D: 0IU, Omega-3: 0.1g*

Chickpea and Vegetable Stir-Fry

Servings: 4

1 can chickpeas (15 oz), rinsed

2 cups mixed vegetables (bell pepper, broccoli)

2 tbsp soy sauce

1 tbsp sesame oil

2 garlic cloves, minced

Drain and rinse the chickpeas in a colander and set aside.

Heat sesame oil in a large skillet or wok over medium heat.

Add the minced garlic and stir-fry for about 1 minute until fragrant.

Add the mixed vegetables to the skillet and stir-fry for 5-7 minutes until they are tender-crisp.

Stir in the chickpeas and soy sauce, mixing well to combine.

Cook for another 2-3 minutes until the chickpeas are heated through.

Serve hot.

Nutritional Information per serving: *Calories: 250, Protein: 10g, Fiber: 8g, Calcium: 60mg, Magnesium: 45mg, Vit B6: 0.2mg, Vit B9: 70mcg, Vit B12: 0mcg, Vit C: 30mg, Vit D: 0IU, Omega-3: 0.1g*

Chili Lime Mahi Mahi

Servings: 4

4 mahi mahi fillets

2 tbsp olive oil

Juice of 2 limes

1 tsp chili powder

½ tsp cumin

Salt and pepper to taste

In a small bowl, mix together the lime juice, olive oil, chili powder, cumin, salt, and pepper.

Marinate the mahi mahi fillets in the mixture for at least 15 minutes.

Heat a skillet over medium-high heat. Add the marinated fillets and cook for 4-5 minutes per side, or until the fish is opaque and flakes easily with a fork.

Serve hot, garnished with lime wedges and fresh cilantro.

Nutritional Information per serving: *Calories: 250, Protein: 30g, Fiber: 0g, Calcium: 30mg, Magnesium: 40mg, Vit B6: 0.3mg, Vit B9: 5mcg, Vit B12: 1.5mcg, Vit C: 15mg, Vit D: 500IU, Omega-3: 0.4g*

Cilantro Lime Rice Bowl

Servings: 4

1 cup brown rice, cooked

1 can black beans (15 oz), rinsed

½ cup corn

¼ cup cilantro, chopped

2 tbsp lime juice

Salt to taste

In a large bowl, combine the cooked brown rice, black beans, corn, cilantro, and lime juice.

Mix gently to combine all ingredients evenly.

Season with salt to taste.

Serve chilled or at room temperature.

Nutritional Information per serving: *Calories: 280, Protein: 10g, Fiber: 9g, Calcium: 60mg, Magnesium: 40mg, Vit B6: 0.2mg, Vit B9: 70mcg, Vit B12: 0mcg, Vit C: 15mg, Vit D: 0IU, Omega-3: 0.1g*

Garlic Butter Tilapia

Servings: 4

4 tilapia fillets

3 tbsp unsalted butter, melted

2 cloves garlic, minced

1 tbsp fresh parsley, chopped

Salt and pepper to taste

Preheat your oven to 400°F (200°C).

Place the tilapia fillets in a baking dish.

In a small bowl, mix the melted butter with minced garlic and parsley.

Pour the garlic butter mixture over the tilapia fillets and season with salt and pepper.

Bake for 12-15 minutes, or until the fish is opaque and flakes easily with a fork.

Serve hot, garnished with a lemon wedge.

Nutritional Information per serving: *Calories: 230, Protein: 25g, Fiber: 0g, Calcium: 20mg, Magnesium: 30mg, Vit B6: 0.3mg, Vit B9: 5mcg, Vit B12: 1.2mcg, Vit C: 2mg, Vit D: 400IU, Omega-3: 0.4g*

Greek Quinoa Bowl

Servings: 4

1 cup quinoa, cooked

1 cucumber, diced

1 cup cherry tomatoes, halved

¼ cup feta cheese

2 tbsp olive oil

1 lemon, juiced

Salt and pepper to taste

Prepare the quinoa according to package instructions and allow it to cool.

In a large mixing bowl, combine the cooked quinoa, diced cucumber, cherry tomatoes, and feta cheese.

Drizzle with olive oil and lemon juice.

Toss the mixture gently until everything is well combined.

Season with salt and pepper to taste.

Serve chilled or at room temperature

Nutritional Information per serving: *Calories: 300, Protein: 12g, Fiber: 6g, Calcium: 150mg, Magnesium: 60mg, Vit B6: 0.2mg, Vit B9: 30mcg, Vit B12: 0.5mcg, Vit C: 25mg, Vit D: 0IU, Omega-3: 0.1g*

Lentil Soup Extravaganza

Servings: 6

1 cup lentils

1 onion, chopped

2 carrots, diced

2 celery stalks, diced

4 cups vegetable broth

1 can diced tomatoes (15 oz)

1 tsp cumin

Rinse the lentils in cold water and set them aside.

In a large pot, sauté the chopped onion, carrots, and celery over medium heat until they soften, about 5-7 minutes.

Add the cumin and cook for an additional minute until fragrant.

Pour in the vegetable broth and bring it to a boil.

Stir in the lentils and diced tomatoes, then reduce the heat to low.

Cover and simmer for about 30-35 minutes, or until the lentils are tender.

Adjust seasoning with salt and pepper if desired and serve hot.

Nutritional Information per serving: *Calories: 180, Protein: 12g, Fiber: 10g, Calcium: 80mg, Magnesium: 40mg, Vit B6: 0.3mg, Vit B9: 90mcg, Vit B12: 0mcg, Vit C: 15mg, Vit D: 0IU, Omega-3: 0.1g*

Meatless Stuffed Bell Peppers

Servings: 4

4 bell peppers

1 cup cooked quinoa

1 can black beans (15 oz), rinsed

1 cup corn

1 tsp cumin

½ cup salsa

Preheat your oven to 375°F (190°C).

Cut the tops off the bell peppers and remove the seeds. Place them in a baking dish.

In a mixing bowl, combine the cooked quinoa, black beans, corn, cumin, and salsa. Stir until mixed.

Stuff each bell pepper generously with the quinoa mixture.

Cover the baking dish with foil and bake for 30 minutes.

Remove the foil for the last 10 minutes of baking to allow the tops to brown slightly.

Serve warm.

Nutritional Information per serving: *Calories: 220, Protein: 10g, Fiber: 9g, Calcium: 60mg, Magnesium: 50mg, Vit B6: 0.2mg, Vit B9: 80mcg, Vit B12: 0mcg, Vit C: 35mg, Vit D: 0IU, Omega-3: 0.1g*

Mediterranean Baked Cod

Servings: 4

4 cod fillets

1 cup cherry tomatoes, halved

¼ cup Kalamata olives, pitted and sliced

2 tbsp olive oil

1 tbsp capers, drained

1 tsp dried oregano

Salt and pepper to taste

Preheat your oven to 375°F (190°C).

Place the cod fillets in a baking dish and scatter the cherry tomatoes, olives, and capers around them.

Drizzle olive oil over the fish and vegetables, and season with oregano, salt, and pepper.

Bake for 20-25 minutes, or until the cod is cooked through and flakes easily with a fork.

Serve hot, garnished with fresh parsley or a lemon wedge.

Nutritional Information per serving: *Calories: 200, Protein: 25g, Fiber: 2g, Calcium: 40mg, Magnesium: 45mg, Vit B6: 0.3mg, Vit B9: 10mcg, Vit B12: 1.5mcg, Vit C: 15mg, Vit D: 300IU, Omega-3: 0.3g*

Mushroom and Spinach Risotto

Servings: 4

1 cup arborio rice

4 cups vegetable broth

2 cups mushrooms, sliced

2 cups spinach, fresh

1 onion, chopped

¼ cup Parmesan cheese

2 tbsp olive oil

In a pot, heat the olive oil over medium heat.

Add the chopped onion and sauté until translucent, about 5 minutes.

Add the sliced mushrooms and cook until soft, about 5-7 minutes.

Stir in the arborio rice and cook for 2 minutes, stirring frequently.

Gradually add the vegetable broth, one cup at a time, stirring until absorbed before adding more.

Once the rice is al dente (about 20 minutes), stir in the fresh spinach and Parmesan cheese.

Serve hot.

Nutritional Information per serving: Calories: 350, Protein: 10g, Fiber: 4g, Calcium: 100mg, Magnesium: 30mg, Vit B6: 0.3mg, Vit B9: 20mcg, Vit B12: 0mcg, Vit C: 15mg, Vit D: 0IU, Omega-3: 0.1g

Pan-Seared Trout with Almonds

Servings: 4

4 trout fillets

¼ cup sliced almonds

2 tbsp olive oil

Juice of 1 lemon

Salt and pepper to taste

Heat the olive oil in a large skillet over medium-high heat.

Season the trout fillets with salt and pepper and place them in the skillet, skin-side down.

Cook for 3-4 minutes per side, or until the fish is golden and flakes easily with a fork.

Remove the fish from the skillet and add the sliced almonds, toasting them for about 1-2 minutes.

Drizzle lemon juice over the toasted almonds and pour the mixture over the cooked trout.

Serve hot with steamed vegetables or a side of rice.

Nutritional Information per serving: *Calories: 280, Protein: 26g, Fiber: 1g, Calcium: 50mg, Magnesium: 45mg, Vit B6: 0.3mg, Vit B9: 10mcg, Vit B12: 2mcg, Vit C: 8mg, Vit D: 500IU, Omega-3: 1g*

Pistachio-Crusted Salmon

Servings: 4

4 salmon fillets

½ cup pistachios, chopped

2 tbsp Dijon mustard

1 tbsp honey

Salt and pepper to taste

Preheat your oven to 375°F (190°C).

Place the salmon fillets on a baking sheet lined with parchment paper.

In a small bowl, mix the Dijon mustard and honey. Spread this mixture evenly over each salmon fillet.

Press the chopped pistachios onto the top of each fillet.

Season with salt and pepper.

Bake for 15-20 minutes, or until the salmon is cooked through and flakes easily with a fork.

Serve hot with roasted vegetables or a side salad.

Nutritional Information per serving: *Calories: 370, Protein: 30g, Fiber: 3g, Calcium: 50mg, Magnesium: 70mg, Vit B6: 0.5mg, Vit B9: 15mcg, Vit B12: 4mcg, Vit C: 2mg, Vit D: 600IU, Omega-3: 1.7g*

Quinoa and Black Bean Salad

Servings: 4

1 cup quinoa, cooked

1 can black beans (15 oz), rinsed

1 red bell pepper, diced

1 cup corn, frozen

¼ cup cilantro, chopped

2 tbsp lime juice

Salt and pepper to taste

Rinse the quinoa under cold water and cook it according to package instructions, usually in a pot with double the amount of water. Bring to a boil, then reduce heat to low, cover, and simmer for about 15 minutes or until the water is absorbed.

In a large mixing bowl, combine the cooked quinoa, black beans, diced bell pepper, and corn.

Add the chopped cilantro and lime juice to the bowl.

Toss all the ingredients gently until well combined.

Season with salt and pepper to taste. Serve chilled or at room temperature.

Nutritional Information per serving: *Calories: 290, Protein: 12g, Fiber: 10g, Calcium: 60mg, Magnesium: 70mg, Vit B6: 0.3mg, Vit B9: 80mcg, Vit B12: 0mcg, Vit C: 25mg, Vit D: 0IU, Omega-3: 0.1g*

Roasted Chickpeas and Sweet Potatoes

Servings: 4

1 can chickpeas (15 oz), rinsed

2 large sweet potatoes, cubed

2 tbsp olive oil

1 tsp paprika

Salt and pepper to taste

Preheat your oven to 400°F (200°C).

Toss the chickpeas and cubed sweet potatoes in a bowl with olive oil, paprika, salt, and pepper.

Spread them out on a baking sheet in a single layer.

Roast for 25-30 minutes until crispy and golden, stirring halfway through.

Serve warm.

Nutritional Information per serving: *Calories: 320, Protein: 12g, Fiber: 10g, Calcium: 50mg, Magnesium: 70mg, Vit B6: 0.2mg, Vit B9: 80mcg, Vit B12: 0mcg, Vit C: 30mg, Vit D: 0IU, Omega-3: 0.1g*

Spicy Tuna Patties

Servings: 4

2 cans tuna (5 oz each), drained

¼ cup breadcrumbs

1 egg, beaten

2 green onions, chopped

1 tbsp hot sauce (optional)

Salt and pepper to taste

2 tbsp olive oil for frying

In a mixing bowl, combine the drained tuna, breadcrumbs, beaten egg, chopped green onions, hot sauce (if using), salt, and pepper.

Mix well and form the mixture into 4 patties.

Heat the olive oil in a skillet over medium heat.

Fry the patties for 3-4 minutes on each side, or until golden brown.

Serve hot with a side salad or in a sandwich.

Nutritional Information per serving: *Calories: 250, Protein: 30g, Fiber: 1g, Calcium: 30mg, Magnesium: 25mg, Vit B6: 0.4mg, Vit B9: 15mcg, Vit B12: 2.5mcg, Vit C: 0mg, Vit D: 300IU, Omega-3: 0.5g*

Spinach and Feta Stuffed Portobello Mushrooms

Servings: 4

4 large portobello mushrooms

2 cups spinach, cooked

½ cup feta cheese

¼ cup breadcrumbs

2 tbsp olive oil

Salt and pepper to taste

Preheat your oven to 375°F (190°C).

Clean the portobello mushrooms and remove the stems.

In a mixing bowl, combine the cooked spinach, feta cheese, breadcrumbs, salt, and pepper.

Fill each portobello mushroom cap with the spinach and feta mixture.

Drizzle olive oil over the stuffed mushrooms.

Place them on a baking sheet and bake for 20 minutes or until golden and heated through.

Serve warm.

Nutritional Information per serving: *Calories: 220, Protein: 10g, Fiber: 5g, Calcium: 200mg, Magnesium: 30mg, Vit B6: 0.2mg, Vit B9: 25mcg, Vit B12: 0.5mcg, Vit C: 15mg, Vit D: 0IU, Omega-3: 0.1g*

Spinach and Mushroom Garlic Pasta

Servings: 4

8 oz whole wheat pasta (spaghetti or fettuccine)

2 tbsp olive oil

3 cloves garlic, minced

8 oz mushrooms, sliced

3 cups fresh spinach, roughly chopped

¼ cup grated Parmesan cheese

¼ cup pasta cooking water (reserved)

Salt and pepper to taste

Juice of ½ lemon

Cook the pasta according to the package instructions. Reserve ¼ cup of the pasta cooking water, then drain the pasta and set it aside.

In a large skillet, heat the olive oil over medium heat. Add the minced garlic and cook for 1-2 minutes, stirring frequently, until fragrant but not browned.

Add the sliced mushrooms to the skillet and cook for about 5-7 minutes, or until they release their moisture and begin to brown.

Add the chopped spinach to the skillet and cook for 2-3 minutes, until wilted.

Add the cooked pasta to the skillet, along with the reserved pasta cooking water. Toss everything together to coat the pasta evenly with the garlic, mushroom, and spinach mixture.

Stir in the grated Parmesan cheese, season with salt and pepper, and squeeze lemon juice over the pasta.

Serve hot, garnished with extra Parmesan cheese if desired.

Nutritional Information per serving: *Calories: 350, Protein: 12g, Fiber: 6g, Calcium: 150mg, Magnesium: 60mg, Vit B6: 0.2mg, Vit B9: 140mcg, Vit B12: 0mcg, Vit C: 10mg, Vit D: 1IU, Omega-3: 0.1g*

Teriyaki Glazed Swordfish

Servings: 4

4 swordfish steaks

¼ cup soy sauce

2 tbsp honey

1 tbsp rice vinegar

1 clove garlic, minced

1 tsp sesame oil

1 tbsp sesame seeds

In a bowl, mix together the soy sauce, honey, rice vinegar, minced garlic, and sesame oil to make the teriyaki glaze.

Marinate the swordfish steaks in the glaze for at least 20 minutes.

Preheat a grill or grill pan to medium-high heat.

Grill the swordfish steaks for 4-5 minutes per side, basting occasionally with the glaze.

Sprinkle sesame seeds over the fish before serving.

Serve hot with a side of steamed rice or grilled vegetables.

Nutritional Information per serving: *Calories: 320, Protein: 35g, Fiber: 0g, Calcium: 30mg, Magnesium: 50mg, Vit B6: 0.6mg, Vit B9: 4mcg, Vit B12: 3mcg, Vit C: 2mg, Vit D: 600IU, Omega-3: 0.7g*

Vegetable and Chickpea Curry

Servings: 4

1 can chickpeas (15 oz), rinsed

1 can coconut milk (13.5 oz)

1 cup diced tomatoes (canned)

1 onion, chopped

2 cups mixed vegetables

2 tbsp curry powder

Salt to taste

In a large pot, sauté the chopped onion over medium heat until translucent, about 5 minutes.

Add the curry powder and stir for 1 minute until fragrant.

Add the mixed vegetables, chickpeas, diced tomatoes, and coconut milk.

Stir well to combine and bring the mixture to a gentle simmer.

Cover and cook for about 20 minutes, stirring occasionally.

Season with salt and serve hot over rice or quinoa.

Nutritional Information per serving: *Calories: 350, Protein: 12g, Fiber: 10g, Calcium: 40mg, Magnesium: 50mg, Vit B6: 0.2mg, Vit B9: 70mcg, Vit B12: 0mcg, Vit C: 20mg, Vit D: 0IU, Omega-3: 0.1g*

Vegetable Pasta Primavera

Servings: 4

8 oz whole grain pasta

2 cups mixed vegetables (zucchini, bell peppers, carrots)

2 tbsp olive oil

¼ cup Parmesan cheese

Salt and pepper to taste

Cook the whole grain pasta according to package instructions until al dente. Drain and set aside.

In a large skillet, heat olive oil over medium heat.

Add the mixed vegetables and sauté for 5-7 minutes until tender.

Toss the cooked pasta with the sautéed vegetables.

Sprinkle with Parmesan cheese and season with salt and pepper.

Serve immediately.

Nutritional Information per serving: Calories: 340, Protein: 12g, Fiber: 8g, Calcium: 80mg, Magnesium: 50mg, Vit B6: 0.2mg, Vit B9: 45mcg, Vit B12: 0mcg, Vit C: 35mg, Vit D: 0IU, Omega-3: 0.1g

Vegetable Stir-Fried Quinoa

Servings: 4

1 cup quinoa, cooked

2 cups mixed vegetables (carrots, peas, bell peppers)

2 tbsp soy sauce

1 tbsp sesame oil

1 egg (optional)

2 green onions, sliced

Prepare the quinoa according to package instructions and set aside.

In a large skillet, heat sesame oil over medium-high heat.

Add mixed vegetables and stir-fry for about 5 minutes until tender.

Add the cooked quinoa and soy sauce, stirring to combine everything.

If using, scramble the egg in a separate pan and then mix it into the quinoa and vegetables.

Garnish with sliced green onions and serve hot.

Nutritional Information per serving: *Calories: 220, Protein: 8g, Fiber: 5g, Calcium: 30mg, Magnesium: 45mg, Vit B6: 0.3mg, Vit B9: 50mcg, Vit B12: 0.5mcg, Vit C: 25mg, Vit D: 0IU, Omega-3: 0.1g*

Zucchini Noodles with Pesto

Servings: 4

4 medium zucchinis, spiralized

½ cup pesto

¼ cup pine nuts

¼ cup Parmesan cheese, grated

Using a spiralizer, turn the zucchinis into noodles and set aside.

In a large skillet, lightly sauté the zucchini noodles in a bit of olive oil for 2-3 minutes, just until they are warmed through but still firm.

Remove from heat and add the pesto, tossing to coat the noodles evenly.

Top with pine nuts and grated Parmesan cheese before serving.

Serve immediately.

Nutritional Information per serving: *Calories: 230, Protein: 8g, Fiber: 4g, Calcium: 120mg, Magnesium: 30mg, Vit B6: 0.2mg, Vit B9: 15mcg, Vit B12: 0mcg, Vit C: 20mg, Vit D: 0IU, Omega-3: 0.1g*

GLUTEN-FREE RECIPES

Avocado Toast with Cherry Tomatoes

Baked Oatmeal with Berries

Baked Tofu and Vegetable Bowl

Butternut Squash and Kale Stir-Fry

Cabbage and Carrot Slaw

Chickpea Curry with Spinach

Eggplant and Chickpea Stew

Garlic and Herb Roasted Potatoes

Lentil and Vegetable Stir-Fry

Mushroom and Barley Risotto

Peanut Butter Banana Smoothie

Quinoa and Kale Stuffed Peppers

Quinoa Salad with Black Beans and Avocado

Roasted Cauliflower and Chickpeas

Roasted Vegetable Quinoa Bowl

Spicy Lentil Soup

Spinach and Feta Stuffed Sweet Potatoes

Sweet Potato and Black Bean Quesadillas

Tomato and Cucumber Salad

Vegetable and Hummus Wrap

Avocado Toast with Cherry Tomatoes

Servings: 4

4 slices whole-grain bread

2 ripe avocados

1 cup halved cherry tomatoes

1 tablespoon olive oil

Salt and pepper to taste

Fresh basil for garnish

Toast the whole-grain bread slices until golden.

In a bowl, mash the avocados and season with salt and pepper.

Spread the mashed avocado onto each slice of toast.

In a small bowl, toss cherry tomatoes with olive oil, salt, and pepper.

Top each avocado toast with cherry tomatoes and garnish with fresh basil.

Nutritional Information per serving: 280 calories, 8g protein, 10g fiber, 80mg calcium, 40mg magnesium, 0.5mg Vit B6, 60mcg Vit B9 (folate), 0mcg Vit B12, 15mg Vit C, 0mcg Vit D, 0.1g omega-3

Baked Oatmeal with Berries

Servings: 4

2 cups rolled oats

2 cups almond milk (or other plant-based milk)

¼ cup maple syrup (or honey)

1 teaspoon vanilla extract

1 teaspoon baking powder

1 teaspoon cinnamon

1 cup mixed berries (fresh or frozen)

¼ cup chopped walnuts (optional)

Preheat the oven to 350°F (175°C) and grease an 8x8-inch baking dish.

In a large bowl, mix rolled oats, almond milk, maple syrup, vanilla extract, baking powder, cinnamon, and half of the berries.

Pour the mixture into the prepared baking dish and top with remaining berries and walnuts if using.

Bake for 30-35 minutes until the top is golden and set.

Let cool slightly before serving. Enjoy warm or cold.

Nutritional Information per serving: *280 calories, 8g protein, 7g fiber, 60mg calcium, 45mg magnesium, 0.2mg vitamin B6, 40mcg folate, 0mcg vitamin B12, 15mg vitamin C, 0mcg vitamin D, 0.1g omega-3*

Baked Tofu and Vegetable Bowl

Servings: 4

1 block firm tofu

2 tablespoons soy sauce

1 tablespoon sesame oil

2 cups mixed vegetables (like bell peppers and zucchini)

Cooked brown rice or quinoa (for serving)

Preheat the oven to 400°F (200°C).

Cut tofu into cubes and toss with soy sauce and sesame oil.

Spread tofu on a baking sheet and add mixed vegetables.

Bake for 25-30 minutes, stirring halfway through until golden.

Serve over cooked brown rice or quinoa, drizzled with additional soy sauce if desired.

Nutritional Information per serving: *360 calories, 22g protein, 8g fiber, 100mg calcium, 70mg magnesium, 0.4mg Vit B6, 40mcg Vit B9 (folate), 0mcg Vit B12, 20mg Vit C, 0mcg Vit D, 0.2g omega-3*

Cabbage and Carrot Slaw

Servings: 4

2 cups shredded cabbage

1 cup shredded carrots

¼ cup apple cider vinegar

2 tablespoons olive oil

1 tablespoon honey (or agave)

Salt and pepper to taste

In a large bowl, combine shredded cabbage and carrots.

In a small bowl, whisk together apple cider vinegar, olive oil, honey, salt, and pepper.

Pour dressing over the cabbage and carrots; toss to combine.

Let sit for at least 15 minutes before serving to allow flavors to meld.

Nutritional Information per serving: *130 calories, 3g protein, 5g fiber, 60mg calcium, 30mg magnesium, 0.2mg Vit B6, 30mcg Vit B9 (folate), 0mcg Vit B12, 15mg Vit C, 0mcg Vit D, 0.1g omega-3*

Butternut Squash and Kale Stir-Fry

Servings: 4

1 small butternut squash (peeled and diced)

4 cups chopped kale (stems removed)

1 tablespoon olive oil

1 diced onion

3 cloves minced garlic

¼ cup vegetable broth

Salt and pepper to taste

1 tablespoon balsamic vinegar

In a large skillet, heat olive oil over medium heat.

Add onion and garlic; sauté for 5 minutes until softened.

Stir in diced butternut squash and cook for 10 minutes.

Add chopped kale and vegetable broth; cover and cook for 5 minutes until kale is wilted.

Uncover, stir in balsamic vinegar, salt, and pepper, and cook for another 2-3 minutes.

Serve warm as a side or over grains.

Nutritional Information pe serving: *220 calories, 6g protein, 8g fiber, 80mg calcium, 40mg magnesium, 0.3mg Vit B6, 100mcg folate, 0mcg Vit B12, 40mg Vit C, 0mcg Vit D, 0.2g omega-3*

Chickpea Curry with Spinach

Servings: 4

1 tablespoon olive oil

1 diced onion

3 cloves minced garlic

1 tablespoon curry powder

1 can (15 oz) chickpeas (drained and rinsed)

1 can (14 oz) diced tomatoes

1 cup vegetable broth

2 cups fresh spinach

Salt and pepper to taste

Heat olive oil in a large skillet over medium heat.

Add diced onion and minced garlic; sauté for 5 minutes until translucent.

Stir in curry powder and cook for another minute.

Add chickpeas, diced tomatoes, and vegetable broth; bring to a boil.

Reduce heat and simmer for 15 minutes.

Stir in fresh spinach until wilted.

Serve over cooked brown rice or quinoa.

__Nutritional Information per serving:__ 250 calories, 10g protein, 8g fiber, 70mg calcium, 50mg magnesium, 0.5mg Vit B6, 100mcg Vit B9 (folate), 0mcg Vit B12, 25mg Vit C, 0mcg Vit D, 0.1g omega-3

Eggplant and Chickpea Stew

Servings: 4

1 large eggplant (diced)

1 can (15 oz) chickpeas (drained and rinsed)

1 tablespoon olive oil

1 diced onion

3 cloves minced garlic

1 can (14 oz) diced tomatoes

1 teaspoon cumin

Salt and pepper to taste

Heat olive oil in a large pot over medium heat.

Add diced onion and minced garlic, sauté until translucent.

Stir in eggplant and cook for 5 minutes.

Add chickpeas, diced tomatoes, cumin, salt, and pepper; simmer for 20 minutes.

Serve warm, optionally garnished with fresh parsley.

Nutritional Information per serving: *280 calories, 10g protein, 12g fiber, 70mg calcium, 50mg magnesium, 0.3mg Vit B6, 100mcg Vit B9 (folate), 0mcg Vit B12, 25mg Vit C, 0mcg Vit D, 0.1g omega-3*

Garlic and Herb Roasted Potatoes

Servings: 4

2 pounds baby potatoes (halved)

2 tablespoons olive oil

3 cloves minced garlic

1 tablespoon dried rosemary

Salt and pepper to taste

Preheat the oven to 400°F (200°C).

In a bowl, toss halved potatoes with olive oil, garlic, rosemary, salt, and pepper.

Spread on a baking sheet in a single layer.

Roast for 30-35 minutes until golden and crispy, tossing halfway through.

Serve warm as a side dish.

Nutritional Information per serving: *220 calories, 5g protein, 5g fiber, 40mg calcium, 20mg magnesium, 0.2mg Vit B6, 15mcg Vit B9 (folate), 0mcg Vit B12, 10mg Vit C, 0mcg Vit D, 0.1g omega-3.*

Lentil and Vegetable Stir-Fry

Servings: 4

1 cup green lentils

1 tablespoon olive oil

1 chopped bell pepper

1 cup broccoli florets

1 cup sliced carrots

2 tablespoons soy sauce

1 tablespoon sesame oil

Cook lentils according to package instructions.

In a large skillet, heat olive oil over medium-high heat.

Add bell pepper, broccoli, and carrots; stir-fry for 5 minutes.

Add cooked lentils, soy sauce, and sesame oil; stir to combine.

Cook for an additional 5 minutes, stirring frequently.

Serve warm, garnished with sesame seeds if desired

Nutritional Information per serving: *320 calories, 15g protein, 12g fiber, 60mg calcium, 70mg magnesium, 0.3mg Vit B6, 120mcg Vit B9 (folate), 0mcg Vit B12, 15mg Vit C, 0mcg Vit D, 0.1g omega-3*

Mushroom and Barley Risotto

Servings: 4

4 cups vegetable broth

1 tablespoon olive oil

1 diced onion

1 cup sliced mushrooms

1 cup pearl barley

Salt and pepper to taste

In a pot, heat vegetable broth and keep warm on low heat.

In a skillet, heat olive oil and sauté onion until translucent.

Add mushrooms and cook for about 5 minutes.

Stir in pearl barley and cook for 1 minute.

Gradually add warm broth, one ladle at a time, stirring frequently until barley is tender (about 30 minutes).

Season with salt and pepper to taste before serving.

Nutritional Information per serving: 310 calories, 12g protein, 10g fiber, 30mg calcium, 80mg magnesium, 0.3mg Vit B6, 20mcg Vit B9 (folate), 0mcg Vit B12, 10mg Vit C, 0mcg Vit D, 0.1g omega-3

Peanut Butter Banana Smoothie

Servings: 2

2 ripe bananas

2 tablespoons peanut butter

1 cup almond milk

1 tablespoon honey (or agave)

Ice cubes (optional)

In a blender, combine bananas, peanut butter, almond milk, and honey.

Add ice cubes if desired and blend until smooth.

Pour into glasses and serve immediately.

Nutritional Information per serving: *300 calories, 10g protein, 4g fiber, 40mg calcium, 30mg magnesium, 0.2mg Vit B6, 15mcg Vit B9 (folate), 0mcg Vit B12, 2mg Vit C, 0mcg Vit D, 0.2g omega-3*

Quinoa and Kale Stuffed Peppers

Servings: 4

1 cup quinoa

1 chopped onion

2 cloves minced garlic

2 cups chopped kale

1 can (15 oz) black beans (drained)

4 bell peppers (halved and seeds removed)

Preheat the oven to 375°F (190°C).

Cook quinoa according to package instructions.

Sauté chopped onion and minced garlic in olive oil for 5 minutes.

Add kale and cook until wilted.

In a bowl, mix cooked quinoa, kale, and black beans.

Fill each bell pepper half with the quinoa mixture and place in a baking dish.

Bake for 25-30 minutes until peppers are tender.

Nutritional Information per serving: *320 calories, 10g protein, 12g fiber, 80mg calcium, 70mg magnesium, 0.3mg Vit B6, 100mcg Vit B9 (folate), 0mcg Vit B12, 30mg Vit C, 0mcg Vit D, 0.1g omega-3*

Quinoa Salad with Black Beans and Avocado

Servings: 4

1 cup quinoa

1 can (15 oz) black beans (drained and rinsed)

1 diced avocado

1 cup diced bell pepper

¼ cup chopped cilantro

3 tablespoons olive oil

2 tablespoons lime juice

¼ teaspoon cumin

Salt and pepper to taste

Rinse quinoa under cold water, then cook according to package instructions (about 15 minutes in 2 cups of water).

Once cooked, fluff with a fork and let cool.

In a large bowl, combine the cooked quinoa, black beans, avocado, bell pepper, and cilantro.

In a small bowl, whisk together olive oil, lime juice, cumin, salt, and pepper to taste.

Pour the dressing over the salad and toss gently to combine.

Serve immediately or refrigerate for up to 2 hours.

Nutritional Information per serving: *320 calories, 11g protein, 12g fiber, 70mg calcium, 80mg magnesium, 0.3mg Vit B6, 150mcg Vit B9 (folate), 0mcg Vit B12, 20mg Vit C, 0mcg Vit D, 0.5g omega-3*

Roasted Cauliflower and Chickpeas

Servings: 4

1 head cauliflower (cut into florets)

1 can (15 oz) chickpeas (drained and rinsed)

2 tablespoons olive oil

1 teaspoon cumin

1 teaspoon paprika

Salt and pepper to taste

Preheat the oven to 425°F (220°C).

In a large bowl, toss cauliflower and chickpeas with olive oil, cumin, paprika, salt, and pepper.

Spread on a baking sheet and roast for 25-30 minutes until golden.

Serve warm, garnished with fresh parsley if desired.

Nutritional Information per serving: *250 calories, 10g protein, 10g fiber, 70mg calcium, 50mg magnesium, 0.3mg Vit B6, 120mcg Vit B9 (folate), 0mcg Vit B12, 30mg Vit C, 0mcg Vit D, 0.2g omega-3*

Roasted Vegetable Quinoa Bowl

Servings: 4

1 cup quinoa

2 cups mixed vegetables (like bell peppers, zucchini, and carrots)

2 tablespoons olive oil

1 teaspoon garlic powder

Salt and pepper to taste

Preheat the oven to 425°F (220°C).

Cook quinoa according to package instructions.

Toss mixed vegetables with olive oil, garlic powder, salt, and pepper.

Spread on a baking sheet and roast for 25-30 minutes until tender.

Serve roasted vegetables over cooked quinoa.

Nutritional Information per serving: *330 calories, 12g protein, 10g fiber, 60mg calcium, 70mg magnesium, 0.3mg Vit B6, 100mcg Vit B9 (folate), 0mcg Vit B12, 20mg Vit C, 0mcg Vit D, 0.1g omega-3*

Spicy Lentil Soup

Servings: 4

1 tablespoon olive oil

1 diced onion

3 cloves minced garlic

2 carrots (diced)

1 cup lentils

1 can (14 oz) diced tomatoes

4 cups vegetable broth

1 teaspoon cumin

½ teaspoon cayenne pepper

Salt and pepper to taste

In a large pot, heat olive oil over medium heat.

Add onion, garlic, and carrots; sauté for 5-7 minutes until softened.

Stir in lentils, diced tomatoes, vegetable broth, cumin, cayenne, salt, and pepper.

Bring to a boil, then reduce heat and simmer for 30 minutes until lentils are tender.

Blend if desired for a creamier texture, then serve warm.

Nutritional Information per serving: *250 calories, 15g protein, 10g fiber, 50mg calcium, 70mg magnesium, 0.3mg Vit B6, 80mcg Vit B9 (folate), 0mcg Vit B12, 20mg Vit C, 0mcg Vit D, 0.2g omega-3*

Spinach and Feta Stuffed Sweet Potatoes

Servings: 4

4 medium sweet potatoes

1 tablespoon olive oil

2 cups spinach

½ cup crumbled feta cheese

Salt and pepper to taste

Preheat the oven to 400°F (200°C).

Pierce sweet potatoes with a fork and bake for 45-50 minutes until soft.

In a skillet, heat olive oil and sauté spinach until wilted.

Remove from heat and stir in feta cheese, salt, and pepper.

Once sweet potatoes are cooked, slice them open and fill them with the spinach mixture.

Serve warm, optionally garnished with extra feta.

Nutritional Information per serving: *280 calories, 9g protein, 7g fiber, 100mg calcium, 60mg magnesium, 0.2mg Vit B6, 70mcg Vit B9 (folate), 0mcg Vit B12, 30mg Vit C, 0mcg Vit D, 0.1g omega-3*

Sweet Potato and Black Bean Quesadillas

Servings: 4

2 medium sweet potatoes (peeled and diced)

1 can (15 oz) black beans (drained and rinsed)

1 teaspoon cumin

½ teaspoon chili powder

Salt and pepper to taste

4 large whole wheat tortillas

1 cup shredded cheese (optional)

2 tablespoons olive oil

Salsa (for serving)

Preheat the oven to 400°F (200°C). Toss the diced sweet potatoes with olive oil, cumin, chili powder, salt, and pepper.

Spread the sweet potatoes on a baking sheet and roast for 25-30 minutes until tender.

In a bowl, mash the roasted sweet potatoes and mix in the black beans.

Spread the mixture evenly over half of each tortilla, adding cheese if desired, then fold the tortillas in half.

In a skillet over medium heat, add a little olive oil and cook each quesadilla for 3-4 minutes on each side until golden brown.

Cut into wedges and serve with salsa.

Nutritional Information per serving: *360 calories, 12g protein, 10g fiber, 150mg calcium, 80mg magnesium, 0.4mg Vit B6, 80mcg folate, 0mcg Vit B12, 15mg Vit C, 0mcg Vit D, 0.1g omega-3*

Tomato and Cucumber Salad

Servings: 4

2 cups diced tomatoes

1 cucumber (diced)

¼ cup chopped red onion

2 tablespoons olive oil

1 tablespoon lemon juice

Salt and pepper to taste

Fresh basil for garnish

In a large bowl, combine diced tomatoes, cucumber, and red onion.

In a small bowl, whisk together olive oil, lemon juice, salt, and pepper.

Pour the dressing over the salad; toss to combine.

Serve immediately, garnished with fresh basil.

__Nutritional Information per serving:__ 120 calories, 3g protein, 4g fiber, 30mg calcium, 20mg magnesium, 0.1mg Vit B6, 15mcg Vit B9 (folate), 0mcg Vit B12, 20mg Vit C, 0mcg Vit D, 0.1g omega-3

Vegetable and Hummus Wrap

Servings: 4

4 whole-grain tortillas

1 cup hummus

1 cup sliced cucumbers

1 cup shredded carrots

1 cup baby spinach

Spread hummus evenly over each tortilla.

Layer sliced cucumbers, shredded carrots, and baby spinach on top.

Roll up tightly and slice in half to serve.

Nutritional Information per serving: 300 calories, 10g protein, 8g fiber, 80mg calcium, 40mg magnesium, 0.3mg Vit B6, 60mcg Vit B9 (folate), 0mcg Vit B12, 10mg Vit C, 0mcg Vit D, 0.1g omega-3

DAIRY-FREE RECIPES

Almond Butter and Banana Toast

Avocado Toast

Banana Oatmeal Cookies

Beetroot Salad

Cauliflower Rice Stir-Fry

Fruit and Nut Energy Balls

Green Smoothie

Hummus and Veggie Platter

Lentil Soup Soirée

Mango and Spinach Smoothie

Mediterranean Chicken Skewers

Oven-Baked Falafel

Pumpkin Soup

Quinoa and Black Bean Bowl

Quinoa Salad

Roasted Vegetable Medley

Spinach and Chickpea Salad

Stuffed Bell Peppers

Vegan Chili

Zucchini Noodles with Marinara

Almond Butter and Banana Toast

Servings: 2

2 slices whole-grain bread

2 tablespoons almond butter

1 banana, sliced

1 tablespoon chia seeds

Honey or maple syrup (optional)

Toast the slices of whole-grain bread until golden brown.

Spread almond butter evenly over each slice.

Top with sliced banana and sprinkle chia seeds on top.

Drizzle with honey or maple syrup if desired.

Serve immediately.

Nutritional Information per serving: *Calories: 290, Protein: 8g, Fiber: 7g, Calcium: 80mg, Magnesium: 70mg, Vit B6: 0.2mg, Vit B9: 20µg, Vit B12: 0µg, Vit C: 2mg, Vit D: 0µg, Omega-3 Fatty Acids: 0.2g*

Avocado Toast

Servings: 2

2 slices whole-grain bread

1 ripe avocado

Juice of ½ lemon

Salt and pepper to taste

Red pepper flakes (optional)

Toast the slices of whole-grain bread until golden brown.

In a bowl, mash the ripe avocado with lemon juice, salt, and pepper.

Spread the mashed avocado evenly on each slice of toast.

Sprinkle with red pepper flakes if desired and serve immediately.

Nutritional Information per serving: *Calories: 220, Protein: 6g, Fiber: 8g, Calcium: 30mg, Magnesium: 40mg, Vit B6: 0.2mg, Vit B9: 60µg, Vit B12: 0µg, Vit C: 15mg, Vit D: 0µg, Omega-3 Fatty Acids: 0.1g*

Banana Oatmeal Cookies

Servings: 12

2 ripe bananas, mashed

1 cup rolled oats

¼ cup almond butter

1 teaspoon cinnamon

½ cup raisins (optional)

Preheat the oven to 350°F (175°C).

In a bowl, mix together mashed bananas, oats, almond butter, cinnamon, and raisins.

Drop spoonfuls of the mixture onto a baking sheet lined with parchment paper.

Bake for 10-12 minutes until lightly golden.

Allow to cool before serving.

Nutritional Information per cookie: *Calories: 90, Protein: 2g, Fiber: 2g, Calcium: 20mg, Magnesium: 30mg, Vit B6: 0.1mg, Vit B9: 10µg, Vit B12: 0µg, Vit C: 2mg, Vit D: 0µg, Omega-3 Fatty Acids: 0.1g*

Beetroot Salad

Servings: 4

2 cups cooked beets, diced

2 cups arugula

¼ cup walnuts, chopped

2 tablespoons balsamic vinegar

Salt and pepper to taste

In a large bowl, combine diced beets, arugula, and walnuts.

Drizzle with balsamic vinegar and season with salt and pepper.

Toss gently to combine.

Serve immediately or chill before serving.

Nutritional Information (per serving): Calories: 150, Protein: 4g, Fiber: 5g, Calcium: 40mg, Magnesium: 30mg, Vit B6: 0.2mg, Vit B9: 80µg, Vit B12: 0µg, Vit C: 15mg, Vit D: 0µg, Omega-3 Fatty Acids: 0.1g

Cauliflower Rice Stir-Fry

Servings: 4

1 head cauliflower, riced

1 cup mixed vegetables (carrots, peas, bell pepper)

2 tablespoons soy sauce

1 tablespoon sesame oil

2 green onions, chopped

In a skillet, heat sesame oil over medium heat.

Add mixed vegetables and sauté for 5 minutes.

Stir in cauliflower rice and soy sauce; cook for another 5-7 minutes until cauliflower is tender.

Garnish with chopped green onions before serving.

Nutritional Information per serving: *Calories: 100, Protein: 4g, Fiber: 3g, Calcium: 30mg, Magnesium: 20mg, Vit B6: 0.2mg, Vit B9: 30µg, Vit B12: 0µg, Vit C: 40mg, Vit D: 0µg, Omega-3 Fatty Acids: 0g*

Fruit and Nut Energy Balls

Servings: 12

1 cup dates, pitted

½ cup almonds

½ cup walnuts

¼ cup coconut flakes

1 tablespoon chia seeds

In a food processor, combine all ingredients and pulse until a sticky mixture forms.

Roll mixture into small balls and place on a baking sheet.

Refrigerate for 30 minutes to firm up.

Store in an airtight container.

Nutritional Information per serving: *Calories: 120, Protein: 3g, Fiber: 3g, Calcium: 30mg, Magnesium: 40mg, Vit B6: 0.1mg, Vit B9: 10μg, Vit B12: 0μg, Vit C: 1mg, Vit D: 0μg, Omega-3 Fatty Acids: 0.2g*

Green Smoothie

Servings: 1

1 banana

1 cup spinach

1 cup almond milk

1 tablespoon almond butter

1 tablespoon chia seeds

In a blender, combine banana, spinach, almond milk, almond butter, and chia seeds.

Blend until smooth, adding more almond milk if necessary for desired consistency.

Pour into a glass and enjoy immediately.

Nutritional Information per serving: *Calories: 300, Protein: 8g, Fiber: 7g, Calcium: 250mg, Magnesium: 60mg, Vit B6: 0.4mg, Vit B9: 30µg, Vit B12: 0µg, Vit C: 15mg, Vit D: 0µg, Omega-3 Fatty Acids: 1g*

Hummus and Veggie Platter

Servings: 4

1 can chickpeas, rinsed and drained

2 tablespoons tahini

2 tablespoons lemon juice

1 clove garlic, minced

Olive oil

Assorted raw vegetables (carrots, cucumbers, bell peppers)

In a food processor, combine chickpeas, tahini, lemon juice, garlic, and a drizzle of olive oil.

Blend until smooth, adding water if necessary to reach desired consistency.

Serve hummus with an assortment of raw vegetables for dipping.

Nutritional Information per serving: *Calories: 180, Protein: 6g, Fiber: 5g, Calcium: 40mg, Magnesium: 50mg, Vit B6: 0.2mg, Vit B9: 40µg, Vit B12: 0µg, Vit C: 30mg, Vit D: 0µg, Omega-3 Fatty Acids: 0g*

Lentil Soup Soirée

Servings: 6

1 tablespoon olive oil

1 onion, chopped

2 carrots, diced

2 celery stalks, diced

3 cloves garlic, minced

1 cup dried lentils

6 cups vegetable broth

1 can diced tomatoes

1 teaspoon cumin

Salt and pepper to taste

In a large pot, heat olive oil over medium heat.

Sauté onion, carrots, and celery until softened.

Add garlic and cook for 1 minute.

Stir in lentils, vegetable broth, diced tomatoes, cumin, salt, and pepper.

Bring to a boil, then reduce heat and simmer for 30 minutes until lentils are tender.

Nutritional Information per serving: *Calories: 180, Protein: 10g, Fiber: 8g, Calcium: 60mg, Magnesium: 70mg, Vit B6: 0.3mg, Vit B9: 70µg, Vit B12: 0µg, Vit C: 5mg, Vit D: 0µg, Omega-3 Fatty Acids: 0.1g*

Mango and Spinach Smoothie

Servings: 2

1 cup fresh spinach

1 ripe mango, peeled and diced

1 banana

1 cup almond milk

1 tablespoon flaxseeds

In a blender, combine fresh spinach, mango, banana, almond milk, and flaxseeds.

Blend until smooth and creamy.

Pour into glasses and serve immediately.

Nutritional Information per serving: *Calories: 180, Protein: 4g, Fiber: 5g, Calcium: 300mg, Magnesium: 60mg, Vit B6: 0.2mg, Vit B9: 40µg, Vit B12: 0µg, Vit C: 40mg, Vit D: 0µg, Omega-3 Fatty Acids: 1g*

Mediterranean Chicken Skewers

Servings: 4

1.5 pounds boneless, skinless chicken breasts, cut into 1-inch cubes

¼ cup olive oil

Juice of 1 lemon

3 cloves garlic, minced

1 tablespoon dried oregano

1 teaspoon smoked paprika

Salt and pepper to taste

1 cup cherry tomatoes

1 bell pepper, cut into chunks

1 red onion, cut into chunks

Wooden or metal skewers

In a large bowl, whisk together olive oil, lemon juice, minced garlic, oregano, smoked paprika, salt, and pepper.

Add the chicken cubes to the marinade and toss to coat. Cover and marinate in the refrigerator for at least 30 minutes, or up to 2 hours for more flavor.

Preheat the grill to medium-high heat.

While the grill is heating, soak wooden skewers in water for 15-20 minutes if using.

Thread the marinated chicken onto the skewers, alternating with cherry tomatoes, bell pepper chunks, and red onion chunks.

Place the skewers on the grill and cook for 10-12 minutes, turning occasionally, until the chicken is cooked through and has grill marks.

Remove from the grill and let rest for a few minutes before serving.

Nutritional Information per skewer: *Calories: 220, Protein: 30g, Fiber: 2g, Calcium: 30mg, Magnesium: 25mg, Vit B6: 0.5mg, Vit B9: 5µg, Vit B12: 0µg, Vit C: 15mg, Vit D: 0µg, Omega-3 Fatty Acids: 0g*

Oven-Baked Falafel

Servings: 4

1 can chickpeas, rinsed and drained

½ onion, chopped

2 cloves garlic, minced

1 tablespoon parsley

1 teaspoon cumin

Salt and pepper to taste

Preheat the oven to 400°F (200°C).

In a food processor, combine chickpeas, onion, garlic, parsley, cumin, salt, and pepper.

Pulse until the mixture is well combined but still chunky.

Form mixture into small patties and place on a baking sheet lined with parchment paper.

Bake for 25-30 minutes, flipping halfway, until golden brown.

Nutritional Information per serving: *Calories: 180, Protein: 7g, Fiber: 5g, Calcium: 40mg, Magnesium: 30mg, Vit B6: 0.2mg, Vit B9: 70µg, Vit B12: 0µg, Vit C: 5mg, Vit D: 0µg, Omega-3 Fatty Acids: 0.1g*

Pumpkin Soup

Servings: 4

1 can pumpkin puree

1 onion, chopped

2 cloves garlic, minced

3 cups vegetable broth

1 teaspoon cinnamon

Salt and pepper to taste

In a pot, sauté onion and garlic until soft.

Add pumpkin puree, vegetable broth, cinnamon, salt, and pepper.

Bring to a boil, then reduce heat and simmer for 20 minutes.

Use an immersion blender to puree the soup until smooth.

Serve warm.

Nutritional Information per serving: *Calories: 150, Protein: 3g, Fiber: 5g, Calcium: 30mg, Magnesium: 40mg, Vit B6: 0.1mg, Vit B9: 30µg, Vit B12: 0µg, Vit C: 10mg, Vit D: 0µg, Omega-3 Fatty Acids: 0g*

Quinoa and Black Bean Bowl

Servings: 4

1 cup cooked quinoa

1 can black beans, rinsed and drained

1 cup corn

1 avocado, diced

¼ cup lime juice

Salt and pepper to taste

In a large bowl, combine cooked quinoa, black beans, corn, avocado, lime juice, salt, and pepper.

Toss gently to combine.

Serve immediately or refrigerate for later use.

Nutritional Information per serving: *Calories: 300, Protein: 10g, Fiber: 9g, Calcium: 60mg, Magnesium: 70mg, Vit B6: 0.3mg, Vit B9: 60μg, Vit B12: 0μg, Vit C: 15mg, Vit D: 0μg, Omega-3 Fatty Acids: 0.1g*

Quinoa Salad

Servings: 4

1 cup quinoa

2 cups water

1 cup cherry tomatoes, halved

1 cucumber, diced

1 bell pepper, chopped

¼ cup parsley, chopped

2 tablespoons olive oil

Juice of 1 lemon

Salt and pepper to taste

Rinse quinoa under cold water.

In a saucepan, combine quinoa and water; bring to a boil.

Reduce heat, cover, and simmer for 15 minutes or until water is absorbed.

Fluff quinoa with a fork and let it cool.

In a large bowl, combine quinoa, cherry tomatoes, cucumber, bell pepper, and parsley.

Drizzle with olive oil, lemon juice, salt, and pepper; toss to combine.

Nutritional Information per serving: *Calories: 220, Protein: 6g, Fiber: 5g, Calcium: 50mg, Magnesium: 60mg, Vit B6: 0.1mg, Vit B9: 40µg, Vit B12: 0µg, Vit C: 20mg, Vit D: 0µg, Omega-3 Fatty Acids: 0.1g*

Roasted Vegetable Medley

Servings: 4

2 cups broccoli florets

2 cups cauliflower florets

1 red bell pepper, chopped

1 yellow bell pepper, chopped

2 tablespoons olive oil

Salt and pepper to taste

Preheat the oven to 400°F (200°C).

In a large bowl, toss the vegetables with olive oil, salt, and pepper.

Spread the mixture on a baking sheet in a single layer.

Roast for 20-25 minutes, stirring halfway through, until vegetables are tender.

Serve warm.

Nutritional Information per serving: *Calories: 120, Protein: 3g, Fiber: 4g, Calcium: 70mg, Magnesium: 50mg, Vit B6: 0.1mg, Vit B9: 40µg, Vit B12: 0µg, Vit C: 60mg, Vit D: 0µg, Omega-3 Fatty Acids: 0.1g*

Spinach and Chickpea Salad

Servings: 4

4 cups fresh spinach

1 can chickpeas, rinsed and drained

½ red onion, thinly sliced

¼ cup lemon juice

2 tablespoons olive oil

Salt and pepper to taste

In a large bowl, combine fresh spinach, chickpeas, and red onion.

In a separate bowl, whisk together lemon juice, olive oil, salt, and pepper.

Pour the dressing over the salad and toss to combine.

Serve immediately or refrigerate for later.

Nutritional Information per serving: *Calories: 150, Protein: 6g, Fiber: 4g, Calcium: 60mg, Magnesium: 40mg, Vit B6: 0.2mg, Vit B9: 30µg, Vit B12: 0µg, Vit C: 30mg, Vit D: 0µg, Omega-3 Fatty Acids: 0g*

Stuffed Bell Peppers

Servings: 4

4 bell peppers

1 cup cooked brown rice

1 can black beans, rinsed and drained

1 cup corn

1 teaspoon chili powder

Salt and pepper to taste

Preheat the oven to 375°F (190°C).

Cut the tops off the bell peppers and remove seeds.

In a bowl, mix cooked rice, black beans, corn, chili powder, salt, and pepper.

Stuff each bell pepper with the mixture.

Place them in a baking dish and cover with foil.

Bake for 25-30 minutes until peppers are tender.

Nutritional Information per serving: *Calories: 220, Protein: 8g, Fiber: 7g, Calcium: 40mg, Magnesium: 60mg, Vit B6: 0.2mg, Vit B9: 100μg, Vit B12: 0μg, Vit C: 50mg, Vit D: 0μg, Omega-3 Fatty Acids: 0.1g*

Vegan Chili

Servings: 6

1 onion, chopped

2 cloves garlic, minced

2 cans diced tomatoes

1 can kidney beans, rinsed and drained

1 can black beans, rinsed and drained

2 cups vegetable broth

2 tablespoons chili powder

Salt and pepper to taste

In a large pot, sauté the onion and garlic until softened.

Add the diced tomatoes, kidney beans, black beans, vegetable broth, chili powder, salt, and pepper.

Bring to a boil, then reduce heat and simmer for 30 minutes.

Serve hot with optional toppings like avocado or cilantro.

Nutritional Information per serving: *Calories: 210, Protein: 10g, Fiber: 8g, Calcium: 80mg, Magnesium: 60mg, Vit B6: 0.2mg, Vit B9: 70µg, Vit B12: 0µg, Vit C: 15mg, Vit D: 0µg, Omega-3 Fatty Acids: 0.1g*

Zucchini Noodles with Marinara

Servings: 2

2 medium zucchinis, spiralized

2 cups marinara sauce

1 tablespoon olive oil

Salt and pepper to taste

In a skillet, heat olive oil over medium heat.

Add spiralized zucchini and sauté for 2-3 minutes until tender.

Add marinara sauce and heat through.

Season with salt and pepper, then serve warm.

Nutritional Information per serving: *Calories: 150, Protein: 4g, Fiber: 3g, Calcium: 40mg, Magnesium: 30mg, Vit B6: 0.1mg, Vit B9: 20µg, Vit B12: 0µg, Vit C: 25mg, Vit D: 0µg, Omega-3 Fatty Acids: 0g*

VEGETARIAN RECIPES

Avocado and Chickpea Smash

Baked Eggplant with Tomato and Basil

Baked Zucchini with Parmesan

Black Bean and Corn Salad

Cabbage and Apple Slaw

Cauliflower and Chickpea Tacos

Cauliflower Rice with Spinach and Pine Nuts

Coconut-Curry Chickpeas

Eggplant Parmesan

Lemon Garlic Asparagus Pasta

Lentil and Carrot Soup

Lentil and Sweet Potato Stew

Lentil and Vegetable Shepherd's Pie

Pesto Pasta with Cherry Tomatoes and Mozzarella

Roasted Brussels Sprouts with Almonds

Roasted Vegetable and Hummus Wrap

Spinach and Artichoke Dip

Spinach and Ricotta Stuffed Shells

Stuffed Bell Peppers with Quinoa and Feta

Sweet Potato and Chickpea Curry

Avocado and Chickpea Smash

Servings: 4

1 can chickpeas (15 oz), drained and rinsed

1 ripe avocado

1 tbsp lemon juice

¼ cup chopped parsley

Salt and pepper to taste

In a bowl, mash the chickpeas and avocado together.

Mix in lemon juice, chopped parsley, salt, and pepper.

Serve with whole-grain bread or crackers.

Nutritional Information per serving: *Calories: 220, Protein: 6g, Fat: 12g, Carbohydrates: 24g, Fiber: 10g, Calcium: 40mg, Magnesium: 40mg, Vit B6: 0.3mg, Folate (Vit B9): 90mcg, Vit C: 10mg, Vit D: 0 IU, Omega-3 fatty acids: 0.1g*

Baked Eggplant with Tomato and Basil

Servings: 4

1 large eggplant, sliced

2 tomatoes, sliced

¼ cup fresh basil leaves

¼ cup grated Parmesan cheese (optional)

2 tbsp olive oil

Salt and pepper to taste

Preheat the oven to 375°F (190°C). Place the sliced eggplant on a baking sheet lined with parchment paper. Brush the slices with olive oil on both sides and season with salt and pepper.

Layer the tomato slices over the eggplant. Drizzle a little more olive oil if needed.

Bake for 25-30 minutes until the eggplant is tender and starting to brown.

Remove from the oven, sprinkle with grated Parmesan (if using), and garnish with fresh basil leaves before serving.

Nutritional Information per serving: *Calories: 180, Protein: 3g, Fat: 14g, Carbohydrates: 10g, Fiber: 4g, Calcium: 60mg, Magnesium: 20mg, Vit B6: 0.1mg, Folate (Vit B9): 40mcg, Vit C: 12mg, Vit D: 0 IU, Omega-3 fatty acids: 0.1g*

Baked Zucchini with Parmesan

Servings: 4

4 medium zucchini, halved lengthwise

¼ cup grated Parmesan cheese

¼ cup breadcrumbs

1 tbsp olive oil

½ tsp dried oregano

Salt and pepper to taste

Preheat the oven to 400°F (200°C). Place the halved zucchinis on a baking sheet.

In a bowl, mix the Parmesan, breadcrumbs, oregano, salt, and pepper.

Brush the zucchini halves with olive oil and sprinkle the Parmesan mixture evenly over them.

Bake for 15-20 minutes, until the zucchini is tender and the topping is golden.

Nutritional Information per serving: *Calories: 130, Protein: 5g, Fat: 8g, Carbohydrates: 12g, Fiber: 2g, Calcium: 80mg, Magnesium: 20mg, Vit B6: 0.1mg, Folate (Vit B9): 20mcg, Vit C: 20mg, Vit D: 0 IU, Omega-3 fatty acids: 0g*

Black Bean and Corn Salad

Servings: 4

1 can black beans (15 oz), drained and rinsed

1 cup corn kernels (fresh, canned, or frozen)

½ red bell pepper, diced

¼ cup red onion, finely chopped

¼ cup cilantro, chopped

1 avocado, diced

2 tbsp lime juice

1 tbsp olive oil

Salt and pepper to taste

In a large bowl, combine the black beans, corn, diced red bell pepper, red onion, and cilantro. Toss gently to mix.

Drizzle the lime juice and olive oil over the salad, adding salt and pepper to taste.

Mix gently, then fold in the diced avocado just before serving to keep it from browning.

Nutritional Information per serving: *Calories: 210, Protein: 6g, Fat: 10g, Carbohydrates: 28g, Fiber: 10g, Calcium: 40mg, Magnesium: 50mg, Vit B6: 0.3mg, Folate (Vit B9): 90mcg, Vit C: 30mg, Vit D: 0 IU, Omega-3 fatty acids: 0.1g*

Cabbage and Apple Slaw

Servings: 4

2 cups shredded cabbage

1 apple, julienned

¼ cup carrots, grated

1 tbsp apple cider vinegar

1 tbsp olive oil

1 tsp Dijon mustard

Salt and pepper to taste

In a large bowl, combine the shredded cabbage, julienned apple, and grated carrots. Toss to distribute evenly.

In a separate small bowl, whisk together the apple cider vinegar, olive oil, Dijon mustard, salt, and pepper until the dressing is emulsified.

Pour the dressing over the cabbage mixture and toss well to coat. Let the slaw sit for 10-15 minutes before serving to allow the flavors to blend.

Nutritional Information per serving: *Calories: 130, Protein: 1g, Fat: 8g, Carbohydrates: 14g, Fiber: 4g, Calcium: 30mg, Magnesium: 15mg, Vit B6: 0.1mg, Folate (Vit B9): 20mcg, Vit C: 20mg, Vit D: 0 IU, Omega-3 fatty acids: 0.1g*

Cauliflower and Chickpea Tacos

Servings: 4

1 medium head cauliflower, cut into florets

1 can chickpeas (15 oz), drained and rinsed

2 tbsp olive oil

1 tsp cumin

1 tsp paprika

8 small corn or whole wheat tortillas

1 avocado, sliced

Fresh cilantro for garnish

Lime wedges for serving

Salt and pepper to taste

Preheat the oven to 425°F (220°C).

In a bowl, toss cauliflower florets and chickpeas with olive oil, cumin, paprika, salt, and pepper until evenly coated.

Spread the mixture on a baking sheet and roast for 25-30 minutes until the cauliflower is tender and slightly charred.

While the vegetables are roasting, warm the tortillas in a skillet over low heat or in the oven.

Assemble the tacos by placing the roasted cauliflower and chickpeas in the tortillas. Top with sliced avocado and garnish with fresh cilantro. Serve with lime wedges on the side.

Nutritional Information per serving: *Calories: 320, Protein: 10g, Fat: 15g, Carbohydrates: 38g, Fiber: 10g, Calcium: 60mg, Magnesium: 50mg, Vit B6: 0.3mg, Folate (Vit B9): 70mcg, Vit C: 50mg, Vit D: 0 IU, Omega-3 fatty acids: 0.1g*

Cauliflower Rice with Spinach and Pine Nuts

Servings: 4

4 cups cauliflower rice

2 cups fresh spinach

¼ cup pine nuts, toasted

1 garlic clove, minced

1 tbsp olive oil

Salt and pepper to taste

Heat olive oil in a large skillet over medium heat.

Add the cauliflower rice and garlic. Cook for 5-7 minutes, stirring frequently, until the cauliflower is tender.

Stir in the spinach and cook for an additional 2 minutes until wilted.

Sprinkle the toasted pine nuts over the top before serving.

Nutritional Information per serving: *Calories: 160, Protein: 4g, Fat: 11g, Carbohydrates: 12g, Fiber: 5g, Calcium: 40mg, Magnesium: 30mg, Vit B6: 0.2mg, Folate (Vit B9): 80mcg, Vit C: 50mg, Vit D: 0 IU, Omega-3 fatty acids: 0.1g*

Coconut-Curry Chickpeas

Servings: 4

1 can chickpeas (15 oz), drained and rinsed

1 cup coconut milk

½ onion, chopped

2 garlic cloves, minced

1 tbsp curry powder

1 tbsp olive oil

Salt to taste

Heat olive oil in a skillet over medium heat. Add the chopped onion and garlic, cooking for about 5 minutes, until the onion is translucent.

Stir in the curry powder and cook for an additional minute, allowing the spices to become fragrant.

Add the chickpeas and coconut milk, stirring well to combine.

Simmer the mixture for 15 minutes, stirring occasionally, until the sauce thickens. Add salt to taste before serving.

***Nutritional Information per serving:** Calories: 260, Protein: 6g, Fat: 16g, Carbohydrates: 24g, Fiber: 6g, Calcium: 40mg, Magnesium: 35mg, Vit B6: 0.3mg, Folate (Vit B9): 60mcg, Vit C: 4mg, Vit D: 0 IU, Omega-3 fatty acids: 0.1g*

Eggplant Parmesan

Servings: 4

1 large eggplant, sliced into ½ inch rounds

2 cups marinara sauce

1 cup shredded mozzarella cheese

½ cup grated Parmesan cheese

1 cup breadcrumbs

¼ cup olive oil

1 tsp Italian seasoning

Salt and pepper to taste

Preheat the oven to 375°F (190°C).

Sprinkle salt on the eggplant slices and let them sit for 30 minutes to draw out moisture. Rinse and pat dry.

In a shallow dish, mix breadcrumbs, Italian seasoning, salt, and pepper. Dip each eggplant slice into olive oil, then coat with the breadcrumb mixture.

Place the breaded eggplant slices on a baking sheet and bake for 20-25 minutes, flipping halfway, until golden brown.

In a baking dish, layer half of the marinara sauce, half of the baked eggplant, half of the mozzarella, and half of the Parmesan. Repeat the layers.

Bake for an additional 25 minutes until bubbly and golden on top.

Nutritional Information per serving: *Calories: 420, Protein: 18g, Fat: 24g, Carbohydrates: 35g, Fiber: 10g, Calcium: 300mg, Magnesium: 40mg, Vit B6: 0.3mg, Folate (Vit B9): 60mcg, Vit C: 10mg, Vit D: 0 IU, Omega-3 fatty acids: 0g*

Lemon Garlic Asparagus Pasta

Servings: 4

8 oz pasta of choice (e.g., linguine or spaghetti)

1 bunch asparagus, trimmed and cut into 1-inch pieces

2 cloves garlic, minced

2 tbsp olive oil

½ cup vegetable broth

¼ cup lemon juice

¼ cup fresh basil, chopped

Salt and pepper to taste

Cook the pasta according to package instructions until al dente. Reserve ½ cup of pasta water and drain the rest.

In a large skillet, heat olive oil over medium heat. Add minced garlic and cook for 1 minute until fragrant.

Add asparagus to the skillet and sauté for 5-7 minutes until tender.

Stir in the vegetable broth, reserved pasta water, and lemon juice, allowing the mixture to simmer for 2-3 minutes.

Toss the cooked pasta in the skillet, mixing until well combined. Season with salt and pepper, and garnish with fresh basil before serving.

Nutritional Information per serving: *Calories: 320, Protein: 10g, Fat: 10g, Carbohydrates: 50g, Fiber: 6g, Calcium: 40mg, Magnesium: 30mg, Vit B6: 0.2mg, Folate (Vit B9): 60mcg, Vit C: 12mg, Vit D: 0 IU, Omega-3 fatty acids: 0g*

Lentil and Carrot Soup

Servings: 4

1 cup lentils, rinsed

2 large carrots, diced

½ onion, chopped

4 cups vegetable broth

1 tbsp olive oil

1 tsp cumin

Salt and pepper to taste

Heat olive oil in a pot. Cook onion for 5 minutes until soft.

Add diced carrots, lentils, cumin, salt, and pepper. Stir well.

Pour in vegetable broth and bring to a boil.

Reduce heat, cover, and simmer for 25-30 minutes until lentils are tender.

Nutritional Information per serving: *Calories: 180, Protein: 10g, Fat: 4g, Carbohydrates: 30g, Fiber: 12g, Calcium: 40mg, Magnesium: 30mg, Vit B6: 0.3mg, Folate (Vit B9): 180mcg, Vit C: 6mg, Vit D: 0 IU, Omega-3 fatty acids: 0.2g*

Lentil and Sweet Potato Stew

Servings: 4

1 cup lentils, rinsed

1 large sweet potato, peeled and diced

1 onion, chopped

2 garlic cloves, minced

4 cups vegetable broth

1 tbsp olive oil

1 tsp cumin

Salt and pepper to taste

Heat oil in a large pot over medium heat. Once hot, add chopped onion and garlic. Cook for about 5 minutes, stir occasionally, until onion is softened and translucent.

Add the diced sweet potato to the pot, stirring to combine with the onion and garlic. Cook for another 3 minutes.

Stir in the rinsed lentils, sprinkle with cumin, salt, and pepper. Mix everything well to coat the lentils with spices.

Pour in the vegetable broth, increase the heat, bringing mixture to a boil, then reduce to a simmer. Cover and cook for 25-30 minutes, stirring occasionally, until the lentils and sweet potatoes are tender.

Nutritional Information per serving: Calories: 250, Protein: 12g, Fat: 5g, Carbohydrates: 40g, Fiber: 10g, Calcium: 50mg, Magnesium: 40mg, Vit B6: 0.4mg, Folate (Vit B9): 200mcg, Vit C: 15mg, Vit D: 0 IU, Omega-3 fatty acids: 0.2g

Lentil and Vegetable Shepherd's Pie

Servings: 4

1 cup lentils, rinsed

2 cups vegetable broth

1 onion, chopped

2 carrots, diced

2 celery stalks, diced

2 cloves garlic, minced

2 cups mashed potatoes (prepared)

1 tsp thyme

1 tsp rosemary

Salt and pepper to taste

1 tbsp olive oil

Preheat the oven to 400°F (200°C).

In a pot, cook the lentils in vegetable broth for about 20-25 minutes until tender. Drain and set aside.

In a skillet, heat olive oil over medium heat. Add onion, carrots, and celery, cooking for 5-7 minutes until softened. Stir in minced garlic, thyme, rosemary, salt, and pepper, cooking for an additional minute.

Add cooked lentils to the skillet, mixing well. Transfer the lentil mixture to a baking dish.

Spread the mashed potatoes evenly over the lentil mixture. Bake for 25-30 minutes until the top is golden.

Nutritional Information per serving: *Calories: 360, Protein: 18g, Fat: 7g, Carbohydrates: 55g, Fiber: 15g, Calcium: 60mg, Magnesium: 40mg, Vit B6: 0.3mg, Folate (Vit B9): 110mcg, Vit C: 8mg, Vit D: 0 IU, Omega-3 fatty acids: 0g*

Pesto Pasta with Cherry Tomatoes and Mozzarella

Servings: 4

8 oz pasta of choice (e.g., fusilli or penne)

1 cup cherry tomatoes, halved

1 cup fresh mozzarella balls, halved

½ cup basil pesto (store-bought or homemade)

2 tbsp olive oil

Salt and pepper to taste

¼ cup pine nuts, toasted (optional)

Cook the pasta according to package instructions until al dente. Drain and reserve a small amount of pasta water.

In a large mixing bowl, combine the cooked pasta, halved cherry tomatoes, mozzarella balls, and basil pesto.

Drizzle with olive oil and toss to coat evenly. If the pasta seems dry, add a splash of the reserved pasta water.

Season with salt and pepper to taste and sprinkle with toasted pine nuts, if using, before serving.

Nutritional Information per serving: Calories: 400, Protein: 12g, Fat: 20g, Carbohydrates: 40g, Fiber: 3g, Calcium: 250mg, Magnesium: 30mg, Vit B6: 0.2mg, Folate (Vit B9): 40mcg, Vit C: 12mg, Vit D: 0 IU, Omega-3 fatty acids: 0g

Roasted Brussels Sprouts with Almonds

Servings: 4

2 cups Brussels sprouts, halved

¼ cup sliced almonds

1 tbsp olive oil

1 tbsp balsamic vinegar

Salt and pepper to taste

Preheat the oven to 400°F (200°C).

Toss Brussels sprouts with olive oil, salt, and pepper.

Roast for 20-25 minutes, stirring halfway, until browned.

Drizzle with balsamic vinegar and sprinkle with almonds before serving.

Nutritional Information per serving: Calories: 140, Protein: 4g, Fat: 10g, Carbohydrates: 12g, Fiber: 4g, Calcium: 30mg, Magnesium: 20mg, Vit B6: 0.2mg, Folate (Vit B9): 40mcg, Vit C: 60mg, Vit D: 0 IU, Omega-3 fatty acids: 0.1g

Roasted Vegetable and Hummus Wrap

Servings: 4

4 whole wheat tortillas

2 cups assorted vegetables (zucchini, bell peppers, and carrots), diced

1 cup hummus

1 tbsp olive oil

1 tsp paprika

Salt and pepper to taste

Fresh spinach or arugula for filling

Preheat the oven to 425°F (220°C).

Toss the diced vegetables with olive oil, paprika, salt, and pepper on a baking sheet. Roast for 20-25 minutes until tender and slightly charred.

Spread hummus evenly over each tortilla.

Layer roasted vegetables and fresh spinach or arugula on top of the hummus.

Roll up the tortillas tightly and cut in half to serve.

Nutritional Information per serving: Calories: 300, Protein: 10g, Fat: 12g, Carbohydrates: 40g, Fiber: 8g, Calcium: 80mg, Magnesium: 30mg, Vit B6: 0.2mg, Folate (Vit B9): 50mcg, Vit C: 30mg, Vit D: 0 IU, Omega-3 fatty acids: 0g

Spinach and Artichoke Dip

Servings: 4

1 cup fresh spinach, chopped

½ cup canned artichoke hearts, drained and chopped

¼ cup Greek yogurt

¼ cup Parmesan cheese, grated

1 garlic clove, minced

Salt and pepper to taste

Preheat the oven to 350°F (175°C). In a mixing bowl, combine the chopped spinach, artichoke hearts, Greek yogurt, Parmesan cheese, and minced garlic. Stir until well mixed.

Season with salt and pepper to taste.

Transfer the mixture to a small baking dish and bake for 15-20 minutes, or until the dip is hot and bubbly.

Serve warm with crackers or sliced vegetables.

Nutritional Information per serving: *Calories: 140, Protein: 8g, Fat: 7g, Carbohydrates: 10g, Fiber: 3g, Calcium: 100mg, Magnesium: 25mg, Vit B6: 0.1mg, Folate (Vit B9): 60mcg, Vit C: 8mg, Vit D: 0 IU, Omega-3 fatty acids: 0.1g*

Spinach and Ricotta Stuffed Shells

Servings: 4

12 large pasta shells

1 cup ricotta cheese

2 cups fresh spinach, chopped

½ cup grated Parmesan cheese

2 cups marinara sauce

1 tsp garlic powder

Salt and pepper to taste

Preheat the oven to 375°F (190°C). Cook the pasta shells according to the package instructions until al dente. Drain and set aside.

In a bowl, mix the ricotta, chopped spinach, half of the Parmesan, garlic powder, salt, and pepper until combined.

Stuff each pasta shell with the ricotta mixture and place them in a baking dish.

Pour the marinara sauce over the stuffed shells and sprinkle the remaining Parmesan on top.

Cover with aluminum foil and bake for 25 minutes. Remove the foil and bake for an additional 10 minutes until bubbly.

Nutritional Information per serving: *Calories: 320, Protein: 15g, Fat: 10g, Carbohydrates: 40g, Fiber: 5g, Calcium: 250mg, Magnesium: 30mg, Vit B6: 0.3mg, Folate (Vit B9): 70mcg, Vit C: 6mg, Vit D: 0 IU, Omega-3 fatty acids: 0g*

Stuffed Bell Peppers with Quinoa and Feta

Servings: 4

4 bell peppers, halved and seeded

1 cup cooked quinoa

½ cup crumbled feta cheese

¼ cup black olives, chopped

¼ cup cherry tomatoes, halved

1 tbsp olive oil

1 tsp dried oregano

Salt and pepper to taste

Preheat the oven to 375°F (190°C). Place the halved bell peppers in a baking dish.

In a bowl, mix the cooked quinoa, feta cheese, chopped olives, cherry tomatoes, olive oil, oregano, salt, and pepper. Stir until well combined.

Stuff each pepper half with the quinoa mixture.

Bake for 25-30 minutes, until the peppers are tender and the filling is heated through.

Nutritional Information per serving: Calories: 180, Protein: 6g, Fat: 9g, Carbohydrates: 20g, Fiber: 4g, Calcium: 100mg, Magnesium: 30mg, Vit B6: 0.3mg, Folate (Vit B9): 70mcg, Vit C: 60mg, Vit D: 0 IU, Omega-3 fatty acids: 0.1g

Sweet Potato and Chickpea Curry

Servings: 4

1 large sweet potato, peeled and diced

1 can chickpeas (15 oz), drained and rinsed

½ onion, chopped

1 cup coconut milk

2 tbsp curry paste

1 tbsp olive oil

Heat olive oil in a pot over medium heat. Add the chopped onion and cook for 5 minutes until softened.

Stir in the curry paste and cook for 1 minute, allowing the flavors to release.

Add the diced sweet potato and chickpeas, stirring to coat them in the curry mixture.

Pour in the coconut milk, bring to a boil, then reduce to a simmer for 20 minutes until the sweet potato is tender.

Nutritional Information per serving: *Calories: 300, Protein: 7g, Fat: 14g, Carbohydrates: 38g, Fiber: 8g, Calcium: 40mg, Magnesium: 40mg, Vit B6: 0.4mg, Folate (Vit B9): 60mcg, Vit C: 12mg, Vit D: 0 IU, Omega-3 fatty acids: 0.1g*

PASTA RECIPES

Cajun Shrimp Pasta

Caprese Pasta Salad

Chickpea Pasta with Roasted Red Peppers

Creamy Avocado Pasta

Creamy Spinach Pasta

Garlic Butter Mushroom Pasta

Lemon Herb Chicken Pasta

Lentil Bolognese with Whole Wheat Spaghetti

Mediterranean Pasta Salad with Chickpeas

Mushroom and Pea Pasta

One-Pot Spinach and Feta Pasta

Pasta Primavera

Pasta with Garlic Lemon Sauce

Pesto Zucchini Noodles with Grilled Chicken

Salmon Spinach Pasta with Lemon

Shrimp and Avocado Pasta Salad

Sweet Potato and Black Bean Pasta

Tuna and Broccoli Pasta Bake

Vegetable Stir-Fry Noodles

Zucchini and Corn Pasta

Cajun Shrimp Pasta

Servings: 4

8 oz whole grain pasta

8 oz shrimp, peeled and deveined

1 cup bell peppers, sliced

½ cup heavy cream

2 tbsp Cajun seasoning

2 tbsp olive oil

1 clove garlic, minced

Salt and pepper to taste

Cook the whole grain pasta according to package directions.

Drain and set aside.

In a large pan, heat the olive oil over medium heat.

Add the minced garlic and sauté until fragrant, about 1 minute.

Add the shrimp and Cajun seasoning, cooking until the shrimp is pink, about 3-4 minutes.

Stir in the sliced bell peppers and cook for another 2 minutes.

Add the heavy cream and bring to a simmer.

Toss in the cooked pasta and mix until well combined.

Serve hot.

Nutritional Information per serving: *Calories: 490, Protein: 30g, Fiber: 3g, Calcium: 80mg, Magnesium: 60mg, Vit B6: 0.4mg, Vit B9: 50mcg, Vit B12: 1.5mcg, Vit C: 20mg, Vit D: 0mcg, Omega-3: 0.3g*

Caprese Pasta Salad

Servings: 4

8 oz whole grain pasta

1 cup cherry tomatoes, halved

1 cup mozzarella balls

¼ cup fresh basil, chopped

2 tbsp balsamic glaze

2 tbsp olive oil

Salt and pepper to taste

Cook the whole grain pasta according to package directions.

Drain and let cool.

In a large bowl, combine the cooled pasta, halved cherry tomatoes, mozzarella balls, and chopped basil.

Drizzle with balsamic glaze and olive oil, then toss gently to combine.

Season with salt and pepper before serving.

Nutritional Information per serving: *Calories: 370, Protein: 15g, Fiber: 6g, Calcium: 250mg, Magnesium: 40mg, Vit B6: 0.2mg, Vit B9: 30mcg, Vit B12: 0mcg, Vit C: 25mg, Vit D: 0mcg, Omega-3: 0.1g*

Chickpea Pasta with Roasted Red Peppers

Servings: 4

8 oz chickpea pasta

1 cup roasted red peppers, sliced

1 cup baby spinach

¼ cup feta cheese, crumbled

2 tbsp olive oil

1 clove garlic, minced

1 tbsp balsamic vinegar

Salt and pepper to taste

Cook the chickpea pasta according to package directions.

Drain and set aside.

In a pan, heat the olive oil and sauté the minced garlic until fragrant, about 1 minute.

Add the roasted red peppers and spinach, cooking until the spinach is wilted, about 2-3 minutes.

Toss the pasta with the vegetable mixture, add the balsamic vinegar, and season with salt and pepper.

Top with crumbled feta cheese before serving.

Nutritional Information per serving: *Calories: 380, Protein: 17g, Fiber: 10g, Calcium: 160mg, Magnesium: 90mg, Vit B6: 0.3mg, Vit B9: 120mcg, Vit B12: 0mcg, Vit C: 35mg, Vit D: 0mcg, Omega-3: 0.2g*

Creamy Avocado Pasta

Servings: 4

8 oz whole grain pasta

2 ripe avocados

½ cup Greek yogurt

2 cloves garlic

Juice of 1 lemon

¼ cup fresh basil leaves

Salt and pepper to taste

Cook the whole grain pasta according to package directions.

Drain and set aside.

In a blender, combine the avocados, Greek yogurt, garlic, lemon juice, basil leaves, salt, and pepper.

Blend until smooth and creamy.

Toss the cooked pasta with the avocado sauce until well coated.

Serve immediately, garnished with extra basil if desired.

Nutritional Information per serving: *Calories: 360, Protein: 12g, Fiber: 8g, Calcium: 50mg, Magnesium: 60mg, Vit B6: 0.2mg, Vit B9: 90mcg, Vit B12: 0mcg, Vit C: 15mg, Vit D: 0mcg, Omega-3: 0.1g*

Creamy Spinach Pasta

Servings: 4

8 oz whole grain pasta

1 cup spinach, cooked

½ cup cream cheese

½ cup Greek yogurt

1 clove garlic, minced

Salt and pepper to taste

Cook the whole grain pasta according to package directions.

Drain and set aside.

In a large pan, heat the cooked spinach over medium heat.

Add the minced garlic and sauté until fragrant, about 1 minute.

Stir in the cream cheese and Greek yogurt, mixing until smooth.

Toss the cooked pasta with the creamy spinach sauce and season with salt and pepper.

Serve hot.

Nutritional Information per serving: *Calories: 400, Protein: 15g, Fiber: 5g, Calcium: 150mg, Magnesium: 60mg, Vit B6: 0.3mg, Vit B9: 70mcg, Vit B12: 0.5mcg, Vit C: 10mg, Vit D: 0mcg, Omega-3: 0.1g*

Garlic Butter Mushroom Pasta

Servings: 4

8 oz whole grain pasta

2 cups mushrooms, sliced

4 tbsp butter

2 cloves garlic, minced

¼ cup parsley, chopped

Salt and pepper to taste

Cook the whole grain pasta according to package directions.

Drain and set aside.

In a large pan, melt the butter over medium heat.

Add the minced garlic and sauté until fragrant, about 1 minute.

Stir in the sliced mushrooms and cook until softened, about 5-7 minutes.

Toss in the cooked pasta and chopped parsley.

Season with salt and pepper before serving.

Nutritional Information per serving: *Calories: 400, Protein: 12g, Fiber: 4g, Calcium: 30mg, Magnesium: 40mg, Vit B6: 0.2mg, Vit B9: 30mcg, Vit B12: 0mcg, Vit C: 2mg, Vit D: 0.5mcg, Omega-3: 0.1g*

Lemon Herb Chicken Pasta

Servings: 4

8 oz whole grain pasta

2 chicken breasts, cut into bite-sized pieces

1 tbsp olive oil

2 cloves garlic, minced

Juice and zest of 1 lemon

¼ cup fresh parsley, chopped

¼ cup grated Parmesan cheese

Salt and pepper to taste

Cook the whole grain pasta according to package directions. Drain and set aside.

In a large pan, heat the olive oil over medium heat.

Add the chicken pieces, cooking until golden brown and cooked through, about 6-8 minutes.

Add the minced garlic, sautéing for 1 minute until fragrant

Stir in the lemon juice, lemon zest, and chopped parsley.

Add the cooked pasta to the pan, tossing everything to combine.

Top with grated Parmesan cheese before serving.

Nutritional Information per serving: *Calories: 420, Protein: 30g, Fiber: 5g, Calcium: 100mg, Magnesium: 50mg, Vitamin B6: 0.5mg, Vitamin B9: 40mcg, Vitamin B12: 0.2mcg, Vitamin C: 10mg, Vitamin D: 0mcg, Omega-3: 0.1g*

Lentil Bolognese with Whole Wheat Spaghetti

Servings: 4

8 oz whole wheat spaghetti

1 cup lentils, cooked

1 can (14 oz) crushed tomatoes

1 medium onion, chopped

2 cloves garlic, minced

2 carrots, diced

2 celery stalks, diced

2 tbsp olive oil

1 tbsp Italian seasoning

Salt and pepper to taste

Cook the whole wheat spaghetti according to package directions.

Drain and set aside.

In a large pan, heat the olive oil over medium heat.

Add the chopped onion, carrots, and celery, and sauté until softened, about 5-7 minutes.

Stir in the minced garlic and Italian seasoning, cooking for another minute.

Add the cooked lentils and crushed tomatoes, bringing to a simmer.

Season with salt and pepper and cook for 15 minutes.

Serve the lentil Bolognese over the spaghetti.

Nutritional Information per serving: *Calories: 360, Protein: 22g, Fiber: 12g, Calcium: 70mg, Magnesium: 80mg, Vit B6: 0.4mg, Vit B9: 160mcg, Vit B12: 0mcg, Vit C: 10mg, Vit D: 0mcg, Omega-3: 0.2g*

Mediterranean Pasta Salad with Chickpeas

Servings: 4

8 oz whole grain pasta

1 can (15 oz) chickpeas, drained and rinsed

1 cup cherry tomatoes, halved

1 cucumber, diced

¼ cup red onion, diced

¼ cup feta cheese, crumbled

2 tbsp olive oil

1 tbsp red wine vinegar

Salt and pepper to taste

Cook the whole grain pasta according to package directions.

Drain and let cool.

In a large bowl, combine the cooled pasta, chickpeas, halved cherry tomatoes, diced cucumber, diced red onion, and crumbled feta cheese.

In a small bowl, whisk together the olive oil, red wine vinegar, salt, and pepper.

Pour the dressing over the pasta salad and toss gently to combine.

Serve chilled or at room temperature.

Nutritional Information per serving: *Calories: 380, Protein: 15g, Fiber: 10g, Calcium: 150mg, Magnesium: 70mg, Vit B6: 0.3mg, Vit B9: 120mcg, Vit B12: 0.6mcg, Vit C: 30mg, Vit D: 0mcg, Omega-3: 0.1g*

Mushroom and Pea Pasta

Servings: 4

8 oz whole grain pasta

2 cups mushrooms, sliced

1 cup peas, fresh or frozen

2 tbsp olive oil

2 cloves garlic, minced

¼ cup Parmesan cheese, grated

Salt and pepper to taste

Cook the whole grain pasta according to package directions.

Drain and set aside.

In a large pan, heat the olive oil over medium heat.

Add the minced garlic and sauté until fragrant, about 1 minute.

Stir in the sliced mushrooms and cook until browned, about 5 minutes.

Add the peas and cooked pasta, tossing to combine.

Sprinkle with grated Parmesan and season with salt and pepper before serving.

Nutritional Information per serving: *Calories: 350, Protein: 12g, Fiber: 5g, Calcium: 70mg, Magnesium: 50mg, Vit B6: 0.2mg, Vit B9: 40mcg, Vit B12: 0mcg, Vit C: 10mg, Vit D: 0mcg, Omega-3: 0.1g*

One-Pot Spinach and Feta Pasta

Servings: 4

8 oz whole grain pasta

2 cups vegetable broth

2 cups fresh spinach

½ cup feta cheese

¼ cup cherry tomatoes, halved

2 tbsp olive oil

1 clove garlic, minced

Salt and pepper to taste

In a large pot, combine the pasta and vegetable broth.

Bring to a boil, then reduce heat and simmer until the pasta is cooked, about 10 minutes.

Stir in the minced garlic, fresh spinach, and cherry tomatoes.

Cook until the spinach is wilted, about 2-3 minutes.

Remove from heat and stir in the feta cheese.

Season with salt and pepper before serving.

Nutritional Information per serving: *Calories: 380, Protein: 15g, Fiber: 5g, Calcium: 150mg, Magnesium: 70mg, Vit B6: 0.3mg, Vit B9: 60mcg, Vit B12: 0.5mcg, Vit C: 20mg, Vit D: 0mcg, Omega-3: 0.1g*

Pasta Primavera

Servings: 4

8 oz whole grain pasta

1 cup bell peppers, sliced

1 cup carrots, julienned

1 cup zucchini, sliced

½ cup cherry tomatoes, halved

2 tbsp olive oil

1 clove garlic, minced

1 tbsp Italian seasoning

Salt and pepper to taste

Cook the whole grain pasta according to package directions.

Drain and set aside.

In a large pan, heat the olive oil over medium heat.

Add the minced garlic and sauté until fragrant, about 1 minute.

Add the bell peppers, carrots, and zucchini, cooking until tender, about 5-7 minutes.

Stir in the cherry tomatoes and Italian seasoning, cooking for an additional 2 minutes.

Toss the cooked pasta with the vegetables and season with salt and pepper.

Serve hot.

utritional Information per serving: Calories: 350, Protein: 14g, Fiber: 7g, Calcium: 50mg, Magnesium: 60mg, Vit B6: 0.2mg, Vit B9: 80mcg, Vit B12: 0mcg, Vit C: 50mg, Vit D: 0mcg, Omega-3: 0.1g

Pasta with Garlic Lemon Sauce

Servings: 4

8 oz whole grain pasta

¼ cup olive oil

2 cloves garlic, minced

Juice of 2 lemons

Zest of 1 lemon

¼ cup parsley, chopped

Salt and pepper to taste

Cook the whole grain pasta according to package directions.

Drain and set aside.

In a large pan, heat the olive oil over medium heat.

Add the minced garlic and sauté until fragrant, about 1 minute.

Stir in the lemon juice and zest, cooking for another minute.

Toss the cooked pasta with the sauce and add chopped parsley.

Season with salt and pepper before serving.

Nutritional Information per serving: *Calories: 340, Protein: 10g, Fiber: 4g, Calcium: 30mg, Magnesium: 40mg, Vit B6: 0.2mg, Vit B9: 50mcg, Vit B12: 0mcg, Vit C: 30mg, Vit D: 0mcg, Omega-3: 0.1g*

Pesto Zucchini Noodles with Grilled Chicken

Servings: 4

4 medium zucchini, spiralized

2 cups cooked whole-grain pasta

2 grilled chicken breasts, sliced

½ cup basil pesto

¼ cup cherry tomatoes, halved

¼ cup grated Parmesan cheese

Salt and pepper to taste

In a large bowl, combine the spiralized zucchini and cooked pasta.

Toss with basil pesto until well coated.

Add the sliced grilled chicken and halved cherry tomatoes, mixing gently.

Season with salt and pepper.

Serve immediately, topped with grated Parmesan cheese.

Nutritional Information (per serving): *Calories: 320, Protein: 30g, Fiber: 4g, Calcium: 100mg, Magnesium: 50mg, Vit B6: 0.5mg, Vit B9: 50mcg, Vit B12: 0.7mcg, Vit C: 20mg, Vit D: 0mcg, Omega-3: 0.1g*

Salmon Spinach Pasta with Lemon

Servings: 4

8 oz whole-grain pasta

8 oz salmon fillet, cooked (grilled or baked) and flaked

2 cups fresh spinach, chopped

½ cup cherry tomatoes, halved

¼ cup grated Parmesan cheese

2 tbsp olive oil

1 clove garlic, minced

Juice of 1 lemon

Salt and pepper to taste

Cook the pasta according to package directions.

Drain and set aside.

In a pan, heat the olive oil over medium heat.

Add the minced garlic and sauté until fragrant, about 1 minute.

Add the chopped spinach and halved cherry tomatoes, cooking until the spinach is wilted, about 2-3 minutes.

Gently fold in the cooked salmon and the drained pasta.

Squeeze the lemon juice over the mixture, season with salt and pepper, and toss well to combine.

Serve with grated Parmesan on top.

Nutritional Information (per serving): *Calories: 390, Protein: 25g, Fiber: 5g, Calcium: 120mg, Magnesium: 75mg, Vit B6: 0.6mg, Vit B9: 70mcg, Vit B12: 3.2mcg, Vit C: 15mg, Vit D: 10mcg, Omega-3: 1.2g*

Shrimp and Avocado Pasta Salad

Servings: 4

8 oz whole-grain pasta

8 oz shrimp, cooked and peeled

1 avocado, diced

½ cup cherry tomatoes, halved

¼ cup red onion, finely chopped

2 tbsp olive oil

1 tbsp lime juice

Salt and pepper to taste

Cook the whole-grain pasta according to package directions.

Drain and let cool.

In a large bowl, combine the cooked pasta, shrimp, diced avocado, halved cherry tomatoes, and chopped red onion.

Drizzle with olive oil and lime juice, then toss gently to combine.

Season with salt and pepper.

Serve chilled or at room temperature.

Nutritional Information per serving: *Calories: 420, Protein: 22g, Fiber: 6g, Calcium: 30mg, Magnesium: 60mg, Vit B6: 0.5mg, Vit B9: 50mcg, Vit B12: 1.2mcg, Vit C: 20mg, Vit D: 0mcg, Omega-3: 0.5g*

Sweet Potato and Black Bean Pasta

Servings: 4

8 oz whole grain pasta

1 cup sweet potato, cooked and mashed

1 can (15 oz) black beans, drained and rinsed

¼ cup cilantro, chopped

1 tbsp lime juice

Salt and pepper to taste

Cook the whole grain pasta according to package directions.

Drain and set aside.

In a large bowl, combine the mashed sweet potato, black beans, chopped cilantro, lime juice, salt, and pepper.

Toss with the cooked pasta until well combined.

Serve hot or at room temperature.

Nutritional Information per serving: *Calories: 400, Protein: 16g, Fiber: 10g, Calcium: 40mg, Magnesium: 70mg, Vit B6: 0.4mg, Vit B9: 90mcg, Vit B12: 0mcg, Vit C: 15mg, Vit D: 0mcg, Omega-3: 0.1g*

Tuna and Broccoli Pasta Bake

Servings: 6

12 oz whole-grain pasta

1 can (12 oz) tuna in water, drained

2 cups broccoli florets

½ cup low-fat milk

½ cup shredded mozzarella cheese

¼ cup grated Parmesan

2 tbsp olive oil

2 tbsp whole-wheat flour

1 clove garlic, minced

Salt and pepper to taste

Preheat the oven to 375°F (190°C).

Cook the pasta according to package directions, adding the broccoli florets during the last 2-3 minutes of cooking.

Drain and set aside.

In a saucepan over medium heat, heat the olive oil.

Sauté the minced garlic until fragrant, about 1 minute.

Stir in the flour and cook for another minute.

Gradually whisk in the low-fat milk and cook until the sauce thickens, about 3-5 minutes.

Remove from heat and stir in the drained tuna, half of the mozzarella, and the cooked pasta and broccoli.

Transfer the mixture to a baking dish, top with the remaining mozzarella and Parmesan, and bake for 20 minutes, or until golden and bubbly.

Nutritional Information (per serving): *Calories: 340, Protein: 26g, Fiber: 6g, Calcium: 150mg, Magnesium: 60mg, Vit B6: 0.4mg, Vit B9: 80mcg, Vit B12: 2.4mcg, Vit C: 40mg, Vit D: 0.1mcg, Omega-3: 0.3g*

Vegetable Stir-Fry Noodles

Servings: 4

8 oz whole grain noodles

1 cup bell peppers, sliced

1 cup broccoli florets

1 cup carrots, sliced

2 tbsp soy sauce

2 tbsp sesame oil

1 clove garlic, minced

1 tbsp ginger, minced

Sesame seeds for garnish

Cook the whole grain noodles according to package directions.

Drain and set aside.

In a large pan, heat the sesame oil over medium heat.

Add the minced garlic and ginger, sautéing until fragrant, about 1 minute.

Add the sliced bell peppers, broccoli florets, and sliced carrots, cooking until tender, about 5-7 minutes.

Stir in the cooked noodles and soy sauce, tossing to combine.

Serve hot, garnished with sesame seeds.

Nutritional Information per serving: *Calories: 310,
Protein: 10g, Fiber: 6g, Calcium: 30mg, Magnesium:
50mg, Vit B6: 0.2mg, Vit B9: 30mcg, Vit B12: 0mcg, Vit C:
50mg, Vit D: 0mcg, Omega-3: 0.1g*

Zucchini and Corn Pasta

Servings: 4

8 oz whole grain pasta

1 cup zucchini, diced

1 cup corn kernels

¼ cup basil pesto

¼ cup grated Parmesan cheese

2 tbsp olive oil

1 clove garlic, minced

Salt and pepper to taste

Cook the whole grain pasta according to package directions. Drain and set aside.

In a large pan, heat the olive oil over medium heat.

Add the minced garlic and sauté until fragrant, about 1 minute.

Add the diced zucchini and corn, cooking until tender, about 5 minutes.

Toss in the cooked pasta and basil pesto, mixing until well combined.

Serve with grated Parmesan cheese on top.

Nutritional Information per serving: *Calories: 360, Protein: 12g, Fiber: 6g, Calcium: 80mg, Magnesium: 40mg, Vit B6: 0.2mg, Vit B9: 60mcg, Vit B12: 0mcg, Vit C: 25mg, Vit D: 0mcg, Omega-3: 0.1g*

INDEX

A

B

C

E

F

G

O

P

Q

R

Made in the USA
Monee, IL
25 January 2025

10954590R00118